WHEATON 150

In celebration of 150 years

1860-2010

Wheaton College | WHEATON, ILLINOIS

For Christ and His Kingdom

Office of Marketing Communications
Wheaton College
501 College Avenue
Wheaton, IL 60187

Library of Congress Cataloging-in-Publication Data

ISBN 978-0-615-35395-1

Produced by:
Wheaton College
501 College Avenue
Wheaton, IL 60187
www.wheaton.edu
630-752-5000

Designed by Ellen Rising Morris, Eighth Day Creations

Sesquicentennial website at 150.wheaton.edu

Printed in the United States of America
June 2010

Year Verse for Wheaton's Sesquicentennial
One generation will commend your works to another;
they will tell of your mighty acts.—PSALM 145:4 (NIV)

One generation will commend Your works to another

150 years

Wheaton College

est. 1860

Table of Contents

STRETCHED ACROSS WIDE LAWNS WITH TOWERING TREES, Wheaton's campus today bears little resemblance to that of its beginnings in 1860, when a single limestone structure stood on a small hill on the outskirts of a new prairie town called Wheaton. That building housed the Illinois Institute, a college preparatory school established through the determination of Wesleyan Methodist pioneers and the soundness of their enduring ideals.

The Illinois Institute struggled through its short existence. From 1853 to 1859, it welcomed any race or gender to come and learn, but constantly lacked the funds to thrive.

In 1859, Jonathan Blanchard, former president of Knox College, a pastor, and a prominent abolitionist, was invited to assume leadership of the faltering school. The principles of antislavery, temperance, and anti-secret societies on which the school was founded, were dear to Blanchard's heart. "He was like the ocean," Jonathan Blanchard's son, Charles, later wrote. "Stormy and tempestuous, when the winds were raving." He was a perfect fit for the small, inauspicious, floundering college.

The new president was a tireless advocate for Christian higher education and soon persuaded a wealthy local landowner, Warren Wheaton, to make the Institute a gift of 50 acres of land. On January 9, 1860, with approval from the trustees, Jonathan Blanchard renamed the institution after this benefactor.

Thus began the story of Wheaton College.

In the mid-nineteenth century, Wheaton was one of some 200 colleges in America resolved to provide a liberal arts education based on a thoroughly Christian worldview. With the passage of time, America's colleges and universities largely abandoned the Christian perspective as an interpretative framework for the life of the mind. Today, Wheaton is widely known for an unbroken tradition of excellence in the integration of faith and learning throughout the disciplines of liberal arts, athletics, and music.

Wheaton 150 commemorates the sweep of 150 years of the College's struggles, laughter, growth, sorrow, sacrifice, and achievement. Wheaton's mission for Christ and His Kingdom is unshaken and has been strengthened throughout the historic upheavals and conflicts of the past 15 decades. The first chapter of *Wheaton 150* reviews the College's founding vision as it has been upheld and renewed, generation after generation. The history chapter chronicles the programs, people, and events of Wheaton's past and present. The faculty chapter is an affectionate sampling of the professors whose love of students, teaching, and research were and are the bedrock of the College. Wheaton's story continues, featuring campus life, alumni, and a reflection on the future, capturing a panorama of an academic community unswervingly dedicated to Christ and His kingdom.

—Dr. Myrna R. Grant, M.A. '71

Editor, Associate Professor of Communication Emerita

Ever, Only, For Christ and His Kingdom

by Dr. Duane Litfin, Seventh President of Wheaton College

HOW HAS WHEATON COLLEGE COME TO ITS SESQUICENTENNIAL CELEBRATION? No, let's sharpen the question: How is it that Wheaton is still here? A century and a half after its founding, how is it that Wheaton College remains recognizably the same institution, committed to its founding vision?

To a casual observer this question may seem odd. Why wouldn't Wheaton still be here? The rarity of this sesquicentennial celebration could well be lost on such a person. But those of us who are less casual observers know better. We understand the uniqueness of this occasion.

I remember the first time the question of Wheaton's longevity came home to me. It was 1993. We were seated beside one another for lunch, two new college presidents, I of Wheaton, he of another midwestern antebellum liberal arts college.

This new young president had been transparent enough in an earlier session to tell us that his institution was enduring some turbulent times. If he could not help it rediscover its purpose, his governing board had told him, the

school would probably have to close its doors. Now, over our luncheon salads he began plying me with questions about Wheaton.

He was fascinated by Wheaton's founding, its mission and identity, its vision for Christian higher education. He also drew me out about my own Christian commitments and I soon discovered why. His personal religious background was seriously conflicted. He had been whipsawed by his parents between two different religions, he said, so much so that as an adult he had little interest in spiritual things.

Then, with a sudden note of enthusiasm he said to me, "You may be able to help me. My college has a motto and I don't have a clue about what it means. What's more, I've asked all around campus and I can't find anyone

who can explain it to me. Maybe you can help."

"I'll be glad to," I said, "if I can. What is it?"

He said, "For Christ and Humanity."

I realized instantly what I was hearing. It's an all too familiar story to anyone who knows the history of American higher education.

I explained to my friend the meaning of that motto—designed to reflect Christ's summary of the Law. I then counseled him to jettison it, because there was no going back, no way to recover that institution for its founders' intentions. He would have to fashion a new way forward, which that institution has since done.

But I remember thinking then: What about Wheaton? Why is

Our mission endures from generation to generation

Wheaton College exists to help build the church and improve society worldwide by promoting the development of whole and effective Christians through excellence in programs of Christian higher education. This mission expresses our commitment to do all things "For Christ and His Kingdom."

"In the early days slavery was the apparent ruler of our country, and they who would not bow down and worship were crushed when this was possible. This fact explains in large part the life of the college. Though issues change, the great question still remains,—'Who shall reign in this world,—Christ or Satan?' And colleges, like men, take a position on one side or the other. It is the effort of the Trustees, Faculty, and friends of Wheaton College to make it stand firm and true 'For Christ and His Kingdom.' This is the College motto and the College is seeking to be faithful to it."

—Wheaton College Bulletin, *April 1911*

Wheaton still here, still very much committed to Christ and His kingdom? What's different about Wheaton that makes possible not only its survival but its thriving as a Christian liberal arts college?

To this question the ultimate response must be, of course, the providence of God. This is no mere platitude; it's a profound observation about God's preserving grace. But it also forces the next question: What were the *human* means God used to sustain Wheaton for these 150 years?

This answer, I have come to understand, begins with Wheaton's Charter of Incorporation, enacted by the Illinois legislature on February 28, 1861. Wheaton had enrolled its first students over a year earlier, in January of 1860, but the institution was not formally recognized by the state until the issue of its charter. This is the original document under which the College operates to this day.

Wheaton's charter addresses the roles of both the president and the faculty, but it begins by establishing a strong Board of Trustees.

This board, says the charter, "shall have perpetual succession," and, along with other enumerated responsibilities, shall "be impleaded with the power . . . to elect and employ such President, Professors, Instructors and Tutors, for the benefit of said College as they may deem necessary; . . . to fill vacancies occurring in the Board, . . . and [to] do all business that may be necessary and appropriate to secure the permanency and prosperity of the college."

Taken together, the provisions of this charter enable Wheaton's trustees to keep a strong hand on the institutional tiller. If throughout the institution's history this board, being human, has not always managed this role perfectly, for the most part it has done so faithfully and well. For a century and a half Wheaton's governing board has taken its stewardship of "the permanency and prosperity of the college" seriously. Thus, in filling its own vacancies this board has typically, to its great credit, recruited candidates not for their wealth or social standing, but for their grasp of and ability to maintain and contribute to Wheaton's mission. Humanly speaking, this is the backstop reason why Wheaton College is still here, recognizably what it was at the outset.

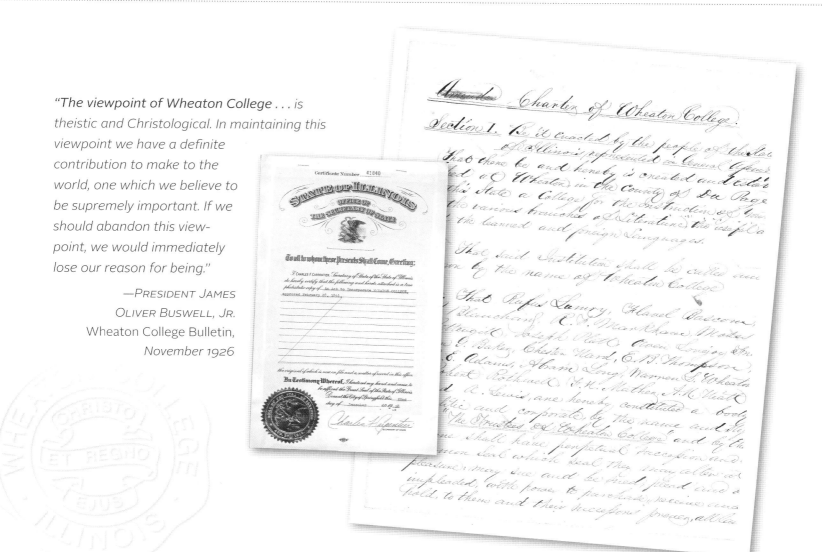

> *"The viewpoint of Wheaton College . . . is theistic and Christological. In maintaining this viewpoint we have a definite contribution to make to the world, one which we believe to be supremely important. If we should abandon this viewpoint, we would immediately lose our reason for being."*
>
> —PRESIDENT JAMES OLIVER BUSWELL, JR.
> Wheaton College Bulletin,
> November 1926

But governing boards can themselves do little to execute an institution's mission. For that they require faculty and administrators. At the next level, then, it must be said that Wheaton is still here because of a succession of administrations and generations of teachers who were hired, not only for their professional qualifications, but for their own commitment to Wheaton's calling. The history of Wheaton College is often told in terms of its seven presidents, and in terms of the hundreds of gifted professors who have given themselves unstintingly for their students. The members of this cross-generational team of leaders were specifically chosen for their ability to further Wheaton's founding mission. To them too, and to the focused hiring policies

that made their gathering at Wheaton possible, must be given much of the credit for why Wheaton is still here.

Then come the thousands of faithful staff members over the decades—secretaries, janitors, managers, coaches, and many others—who were also intent on helping the College hold its course. Then add in the tens of thousands of alumni who were profoundly shaped by their Wheaton experience. These have typically counseled the College to remain faithful to its founding mission for the sake of future generations of students, not least their own children. To this uncounted multitude too must be given credit for Wheaton's longevity.

Finally, there is Wheaton's broadest constituency. These are the innumerable friends of the College who through

their faithful prayer, encouragement, counsel, and support have made it possible for Wheaton to remain what it has always aspired to be. These too have enabled Wheaton to hold its course.

At the human level, all of the above is why Wheaton is still here, recognizably what it was at its founding. Were Jonathan Blanchard to walk onto Wheaton's campus today there is much he would not recognize. He would be astonished by our facilities and our programs and the developments of the twenty-first century. But the longer he looked, the more President Blanchard would, I think, recognize at its core the Wheaton College he founded, a residential liberal arts college that is still here, 150 years later, "For Christ and His Kingdom."

The foundations of our calling

Since its inception, Wheaton's resolve as a Christian liberal arts college has been to "train both mind and heart, and to send forth young men and women well furnished in mind and thoroughly grounded in the principles and practice of an active and reforming Christianity" (*Wheaton College Bulletin,* 1876-77).

Wheaton was the first college in Illinois to graduate African American students, and among the first to graduate women—at the insistence of founder Jonathan Blanchard, who lectured throughout his adult life on the dangers of discrimination and the evils of slavery, intemperance, and secret societies.

Born into slavery in Mississippi, Edward Breathitte Sellers was Wheaton's first African American alumnus, graduating in 1866. Remarkable for his time, Edward earned his bachelor of divinity in 1874; was ordained by the Congregational Church in Selma, Alabama; and served in a pastorate in Chattanooga, Tennessee, with the American Missionary Association.

"The outbreak of the war in the spring of 1861 found myself and two sisters attending Wheaton College, which had a national reputation as an Abolition school in an Abolition town. So strong was public sentiment that runaway slaves were perfectly safe in the college building, even when no attempt was made to conceal their presence, which was well known to the United States Marshal stationed there. With hundreds of others, I have seen and talked with such fugitives in the college chapel. Of course they soon took a night train well-guarded to the next station on the U. G. R. R."*

—*EZRA COOK, a Wheaton student who enlisted in the Union's 39th regiment in September 1861*

"*Wheaton College was established* for the education of both sexes, in accordance with the opinion of the best educators that it is far better that they be educated together."

—Wheaton College Bulletin, 1869-70

"*No distinction is made* as to sex in the courses of study; all students are expected to do thorough work, and will be accredited with the amount accomplished."

—Wheaton College Bulletin, 1876-77

The Class of 1870. President Blanchard's son, Charles, is seated second from the left.

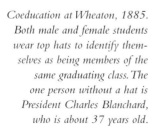

In 1862, Adeline "Addie" Eliza Collins became Wheaton's first female graduate. After graduation, Addie spent three years as the principal of the Ladies' Department (another name for the dean of women). One of her duties included teaching the young women how to handle their hoopskirts. Addie married Henry D. Hatch, and they had one daughter; the family lived on a farm near Addie's childhood home in Will County, Illinois.

Coeducation at Wheaton, 1885. Both male and female students wear top hats to identify themselves as being members of the same graduating class. The one person without a hat is President Charles Blanchard, who is about 37 years old.

From hunting grounds, to homesteads, to higher education

Much like others who platted and populated pioneer outposts in America's West, some hardworking dreamers stopped midcontinent, to settle just 25 miles west of Chicago. There, out of the wild prairie land, a town and a college were born, closely linked from their struggling beginnings until the present.

In 1837 a trio of early settlers from Pomfret, Connecticut—Jesse Wheaton, his brother Warren, and Erastus Gary—claimed for themselves hundreds of acres of land in northeastern Illinois. Wisely, they gave a developing railroad free right-of-way through the growing area. The railroad put up a "Wheaton Depot" sign, giving the community its permanent name. The three founders also gave away land to homesteaders if they would build homes on their new property without delay. In 1859 the town was incorporated. Wheaton, with a railroad running through its center, grew to have churches, a hotel, schoolhouse, butcher shop, post office, grocery store, grain supply, blacksmith shop—and a college.

"Under the trees or elsewhere around Wheaton College there is a far-flung beauty. The old, over-arching forest monarchs rising majestically ninety feet into the air have peculiar loveliness and special significance. For they were planted simultaneously with the establishment of the college. . . . Beneath them wide, winding walks and far stretches of green sward give a college charm for which nothing could substitute. These elms in their strength, their personal beauty, their deep greenness and their restfulness, speak eloquently to the kaleidoscopic student world of the Creator who made the universe and us all who live herein."

—The Light Aloft, *1928*

N. Hale St. Wheaton, Ill.

Wheaton Historic Preservation Council

"It was a little huddle of frame houses on the wind-swept prairie. Many trees had been planted but they were so small as to produce no impression upon the landscape. The ground was low in and about the town on which the water stood the year around. A single building, small, in ill repair and in every way forbidding stood in the midst of a campus which was and is one of the most beautiful spots in the world. . . . As I watch the colors of the trees and see the swell of the ground and look at the sunrise and the sunset and drink in the pure life-giving air, I am always thankful for this place which God seems to have created as a rich educational center for the young manhood and womanhood of our country."

—PRESIDENT CHARLES BLANCHARD, *recalling his first impressions of Wheaton as a 12-year-old in his 1915 autobiography. The school on the outskirts of town was a place this boy would come to revere, and where he would serve a lifetime.*

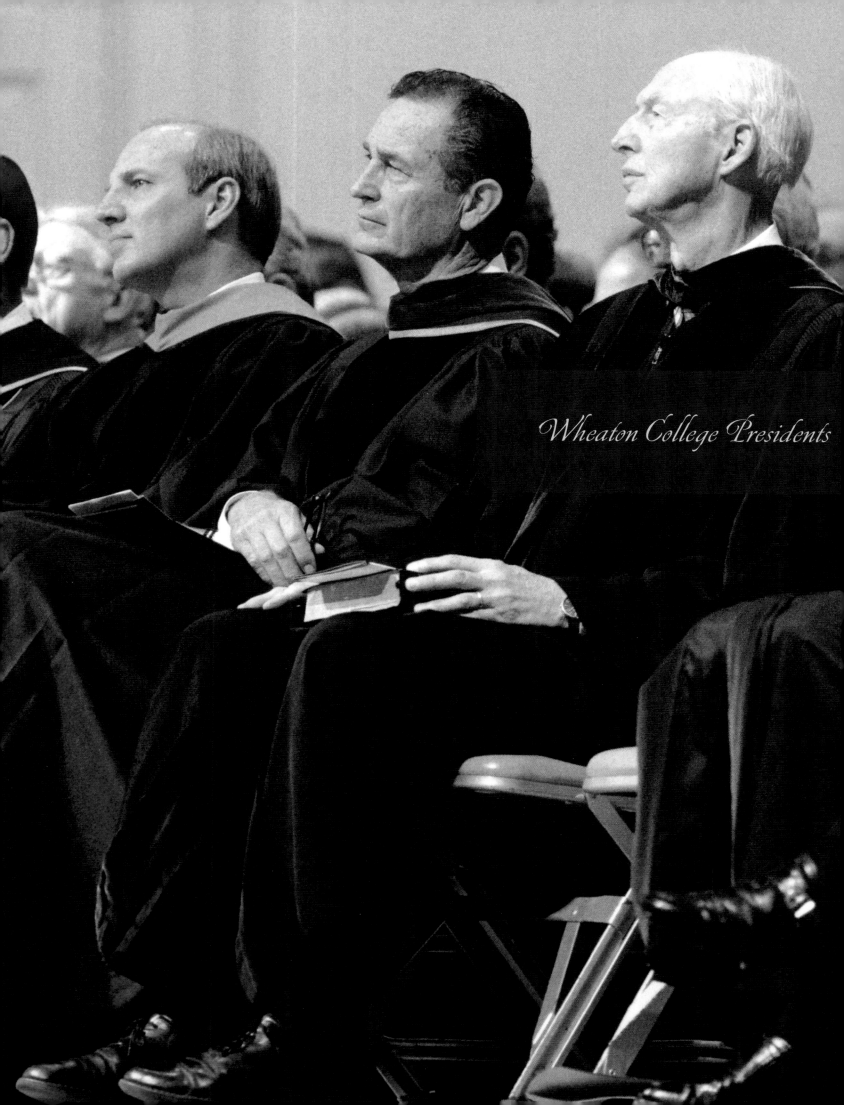

Wheaton College Presidents

Jonathan Blanchard
President
1860–1882

"It is not the books. It is not the books our students read, nor the lectures they hear, nor the laboratory work they do which makes them truly learned. It is the truth which passes into them, and which is sanctified by the Presence of the Divine."

—JONATHAN BLANCHARD, *quoted by Wheaton English Professor Clyde S. Kilby*

"He went everywhere preaching the gospel. . . . He infected both young and old with his lofty ambitions. Young men and women flocked into the primitive town. . . . People who had houses and lands sold them or gave them for the founding of a college in the great valley. . . . With a Bible under his arm, he walked through summer heat and winter cold to humble cabins and little towns, speaking with individuals or addressing meetings, helping people everywhere to be reconciled to God."

—CHARLES BLANCHARD, *describing his father in his autobiography, 1915*

Charles A. Blanchard 1870
President
1882–1925

"The spiritual life of a school is the main thing. It is the end for which all other things exist. Of what value are buildings, equipment, books, apparatus, students, and teachers if the result is not spiritual gain for man and the world? Not only is the spiritual the main thing in College life, but it is the most difficult thing."

> —CHARLES BLANCHARD, stating his vision for Christian education in his autobiography, 1915

"Through nearly half a century he bore the burdens and guided the affairs of the college. He was literally one college president in a thousand, to keep a straight course without deviating from the evident truth of the historical Christian faith."

> —J. OLIVER BUSWELL, in his inaugural address, 1926

James Oliver Buswell, Jr.

President
1926–1940

"Let us base everything upon His grace and upon His glorious message. Upon this basis there is a definite attitude of hope toward life. . . . We all, it is true, may have the feeling of futility, but the Lord will establish the work of our hands for eternity if we but trust in Him and put Him at the center of all we do."

— J. OLIVER BUSWELL, *delivering a 1940 Chapel address*

"It was a shining quality that contributed much to that 'radiant personality,' . . . the ready laugh and high spirits which made him the life of every company, old or young; the heartiness with which he could throw himself into fun and frolic, sport and humor, were always counted on. His illustrations in his talks were often amusing, but we remember them not as entertaining stories, but for their point, marking indelibly many an illuminated text in our Bibles forever. . . . He is an abstract reasoner . . . but, theological and philosophical to his fingertips, he is emphatically a preacher of righteousness, a fearless warrior in the moral battlefields."

—ELSIE STORRS DOW *1881, M.A. 1884, writing of Dr. Buswell in the Wheaton alumni magazine in 1940*

V. Raymond Edman
President
1940–1965

*"It is our privilege to preserve Wheaton's principles—
a Christian education that is truly liberalizing, and we
remember that freedom is a privilege to be deserved,
a responsibility to be assumed, and a duty to be
performed."*

—V. RAYMOND EDMAN, *in a 1947 Chapel address*

*"You may carry with you the satisfaction that you
have left an indelible imprint on this campus,* not only
in brick and mortar and financial assets, but more
importantly, in a strong, dedicated faculty; a staff
of competent, key administrative personnel; and a
student body we can say in all sincerity is second to
none in any educational institution."

—NORRIS A. ALDEEN '38, *corporation president and
Wheaton College Alumnus of the Year 1969 for
Distinguished Service to Society, addressing
Dr. Edman at the time of his retirement in 1965*

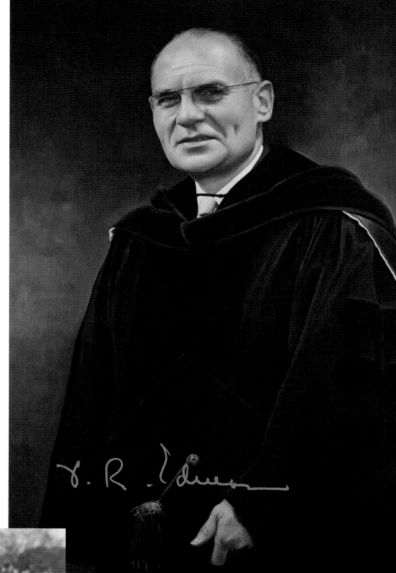

Hudson Taylor Armerding '41
President
1965–1982

"The Christian leader, therefore, should carefully examine himself to identify those characteristics in his life that may interfere with an uncompromising devotion to the Lord Jesus. Then he should be ready to learn from the circumstances through which the Lord might put him. Thereafter, he should continue to grow in perception and understanding so that, as he comes to the close of his life, he may be able out of the richness and fullness of experience and conviction to say to others as Peter said in the last verse of his second epistle: 'Grow in grace and in the knowledge of our Lord and Savior, Jesus Christ.'"

—HUDSON T. ARMERDING, *in his book on Christian leadership,* A Word to the Wise *(Tyndale House, 1980)*

"His whole bearing said, 'I'm not trifling. I'm not going to tell you jokes or entertain you. I am in touch with bigger things.' Dr. Armerding was of the old school of gentlemen, who carried himself a certain way, and was serious about the academic life, about the administrative life, about the life of missions and the church."

—JOHN PIPER '68, *author and pastor, describing Dr. Armerding upon his retirement from the presidency in 1982*

J. Richard Chase
President
1982–1993

"Education has to be more than data and dogma. It has a higher task of developing wisdom, not simply transferring information. It should seek to equip graduates with a worldview, a basic perspective, that will guide and shape the interpretation and use of information."

—J. RICHARD CHASE, *inaugural address, 1982*

"I see you, an admired fellow student, as one who has grown into a carefully disciplined scholar, a learned academician, a strong and creative administrator, a truly Christian gentleman whose power of example far exceeds the authority of your rank, a person above the ordinary, gripped by a mission which you are called to fill."

—GERALD F. HAWTHORNE '51, M.A. '54, *faculty vice chairman, on the occasion of Dr. Chase's inauguration*

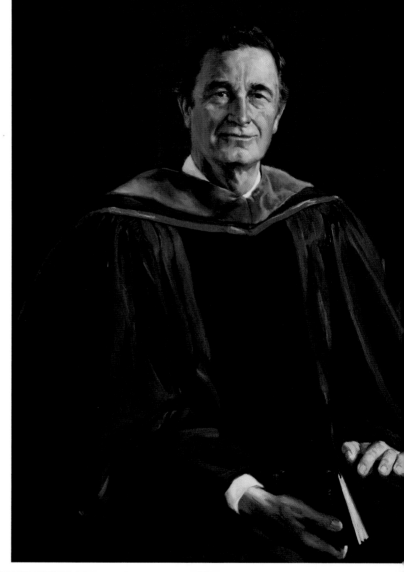

Duane Litfin
President
1993–2010

"In these years to come, we will neither change our banner nor even lower it. We will continue to proclaim with Christians everywhere that Jesus Christ is Lord. We will continue to explore what His Lordship means throughout every area of human learning, every dimension of human experience. . . . We will attempt to live out His Lordship in every aspect of our daily lives by demonstrating to one another and to a needy world a Christlike love for our neighbor, a biblical concern for justice, and a spirit of graciousness to all."

—Duane Litfin, *inaugural address, 1993*

"Dr. Litfin places a profound importance on the Lordship of Jesus Christ. . . . When applied to Christian liberal arts education, this gives a sure foundation for an expansive liberal arts curriculum."

—Gaylen J. Byker, *president of Calvin College, 2004*

Together they led

"Mrs. President Blanchard." So reads the calling card of Mrs. Mary Bent Blanchard, wife of Wheaton's first president, Jonathan Blanchard. Her gift of leadership was apparent as early as age 15, when she became principal of a girls' high school in Montgomery, Alabama. Years later, when Jonathan became ill during his presidency, Mary carried on correspondence for him—letters written in the brown ink of roots and sealed with wax wafers. When Jonathan became discouraged, Mary said, "We finish what we start."

The wives of Wheaton's seven presidents have each brought characteristic strengths to the development of God's work on Wheaton's campus. Each gave to this learning community and its work around the world her own combination of intelligence, vigor, prayer, and generous care.

Together at the inauguration of President Litfin, September 17, 1993: (seated) Miriam Bailey Armerding '42, married to Hudson T. Armerding '41, December 26, 1944; (standing, left) Mary Sutherland Chase, married to J. Richard Chase, December 16, 1950; Sharon "Sherri" Elizabeth Litfin, married to Duane Litfin, July 10, 1965.

(Source: "Romance, Roses, and Responsibility: The Wives of Wheaton College Presidents." Booklet written by Ruth James Cording '33. Wheaton College Women's Club, 1995)

Mary Avery Bent Blanchard
married to Jonathan Blanchard
September 17, 1838

Margaret Ellen "Ellie" Milligan Blanchard
married to Charles Blanchard
October 1873

Amanda Jane "Jennie" Carothers Blanchard, B.A. 1878
married to Charles Blanchard
June 30, 1886

Frances Carothers Blanchard, B.A. 1880
married to Charles Blanchard
February 19, 1896

Helen Spaulding Buswell
married to James Oliver Buswell, Jr.
May 20, 1918

Edith Maxie Olson Edman
married to V. Raymond Edman
June 18, 1924

Jonathan Blanchard said of his wife Mary, "She's my life companion." Mary had a busy life, rearing her large family (not all of her 12 children lived to adulthood) and tending to her four-story home on 20 acres. Professor Darien Straw wrote about living in the Blanchards' home as a student: It "was almost like a hotel—with so many relatives and students." A room on the third floor, which the children were cautioned not to enter, was reserved for runaway slaves traveling to Canada. The pink sweetheart roses that Mary planted in her garden 150 years ago are still flourishing in the front lawn of Westgate, the College's alumni relations building.

Our legacy of leadership

When Jonathan Blanchard accepted the invitation to come to Wheaton College, his one condition was that he would be able to personally gather a group of individuals to guide the College as its Board of Trustees. Through economic crises, denominational disputes, articulations of values and responsibilities, and the growing effects of globalization and technology on higher education, the Board of Trustees has ensured Wheaton's continuity of mission and piloted the College with foresight and wisdom.

1991 Board of Trustees

Row 1: Ruth L. Bentley '55, M.A. '58; George B. Newitt; James M. Lane '52; J. Richard Chase; Gunther H. Knoedler '51; William F. Graham '43, Litt.D. '56; Kenneth T. Wessner '44, LL.D. '90. *Row 2:* Robert O. Hansen '52; Donald L. Meyer '57; Walter C. Kaiser, Jr. '55, B.D. '58; Harold Lindsell '38; Clayton Brown; Jeanne B. Blumhagen; C. William Pollard, Jr. '60. *Row 3:* V. Gilbert Beers '50; David K. Gieser '71; Nathan O. Hatch '68; Harold M. Airhart '61; Alexander Balc, Jr. '61

"Be it enacted by the People of the State of Illinois, represented
in the General Assembly, ... That Rufus Lumry, Flavel Bascom,
J. Blanchard, R. F. Markham, Moses Pettengill, Joseph Platt,
Owen Lovejoy, Freeborn G. Baker, Chester Hard, E. B. Thompson,
R. E. Adams, Abram Long, Warren L. Wheaton, Robert Rothwell,
F. H. Mather, A. H. Hyatt, and A. Lewis, are hereby constituted a
body politic and corporate, by the name and style of "The Trustees
of Wheaton College;" and by that name shall have perpetual
succession and a common seal . . . and do all business that may
be necessary and appropriate to secure the permanency and
prosperity of the college."

—The Charter of Wheaton College,
finalized February 28, 1861

2007 Board of Trustees

Row 1: *Thomas C. Pratt '60; Barbara Wessner Anderson '70; Duane Litfin; C. William Pollard, Jr. '60; David K. Gieser '71; Donald L. Meyer '57; Jeanette L. Hsieh M.A. '66; Kathleen Buswell Nielson '77.* **Row 2:** *Melvin E. Banks '58, M.A. '60, Litt.D. '93; James Plueddemann '65, M.A. '71; Bishop Emery Lindsay; Gary W. Griffin '64; Walter C. Kaiser, Jr. '55, B.D. '58; Philip G. Ryken '88; James A. Bowen '77; Daniel R. Coats '65, LL.D. '92; Gregory S. Campbell '70; Harold M. Airhart '61*

◀ **1940 Board of Trustees**

Standing, l to r: *Thor W. Burtness; Louis L. McShane; Edgar Dival; J. Oliver Buswell, Jr.; George V. Kirk; Charles H. Troutman; Robert E. Nicholas.*
Seated: *David Otis Fuller '25; Alan Emery, Sr.; Henry A. Ironside, Litt.D. '30; William McCarrell D.D. '41; Tom Crofts '13; Darien A. Straw, A.L. 1881, M.S. 1884, Litt.D. 1895; Herman A. Fischer, Jr. 1903*

Our legacy of service

1. **RICHARD GERIG '49** 1958-1989
   Director, Public Affairs

2. **DR. LON ALLISON** 1998-PRESENT
   Director, Billy Graham Center

3. **DR. STEPHEN KELLOUGH '70** 1989-PRESENT
   Chaplain

4. **IVY OLSON '39** 1943-1982
   Librarian; Instructor

5. **BOB NORRIS** 1975-PRESENT
   Chief of Public Safety

6. **GREGORY EVANS** 1999-PRESENT
   Head Athletic Trainer

7. **JEAN RUMBAUGH** 1956-1991
   Administrative Secretary, Academic Records

8. **HEIDI MITCHELL DANIELS '94** 1999-PRESENT
   Assistant Director, Human Resources

9. **DEE AND TO LUONG** 1989-PRESENT
   Day Custodians

10. **SHAWN LEFTWICH** 1988-PRESENT
    Director, Admissions

11. **HOWARD WHITE '41** 1947-1987
    Controller

12. **CLARENCE "C-TRAIN" EDWARDS**
    1979-PRESENT
    Day Custodian; Advisor to Hockey Team

13. **LAURIE LOFTIN** 1999-PRESENT
    *Public Information Coordinator,
    College Ticket Office*

14. **GEORGE V. KIRK** 1929-1944
    Vice President, Finance

15. **DR. EDEE SCHULZE M.A. '89** 1987-2008
    Dean of Student Life

16. **EDWARD A. CORDING '33** 1948-1970
    *Director, Public Relations;
    Director, Music Conservatory*

17. **RUTH JAMES CORDING '33** 1956-1986
    Collection Archival Assistant; Instructor, English

18. **DAVID MALONE M.A. '92** 1991-PRESENT
    Head of Archives and Special Collections

19. **DR. CHRISTOPHER MITCHELL M.A. '86**
    1986-PRESENT
    *Director, Marion E. Wade Center;
    Professor of Theology*

20. **MARJORIE LAMP MEAD '74** 1977-PRESENT
    Associate Director, Marion E. Wade Center

21. **JIM JOHNSON** 1979-PRESENT
    Director, Physical Plant

22. **BRUCE KOENIGSBERG** 1984-PRESENT
    College Architect

23. **STEPHEN MEAD** 1977-PRESENT
    Business Manager

One evening in the early 1900s, a staff member returned to his office on the second floor of Blanchard Hall and found, to his surprise, two men kneeling on his office floor: a janitor and a student. The janitor who had learned of a problem haunting the student was immediately taking it to prayer. Later during Prohibition days George Bushnell, the janitor, evangelized hundreds, including a notorious Spanish rumrunner, wanted for murder.

Wheaton College — 1861

South Western View

A Chronicle of Christian Learning
Wheaton College, 1860-2010

by Mark A. Noll '68, Francis A. McAnaney Professor of History, University of Notre Dame

OVER THE COURSE OF WHEATON'S HISTORY, FRIENDS OF THE COLLEGE and the public at large have identified the school in many different ways. At various times, it has been an institution known for militant opposition to Masonry, alliances with famous fundamentalists, leadership in missionary service, advocacy for "the integration of faith and learning," its striking record of training educators, "The Pledge," the skill of its musicians, and the prowess of its athletes. Illustrious alumni have also defined the College in the public eye, such as Billy '43, LITT.D. '56 and Ruth Bell Graham '43, L.H.D. '75, or Jim '49 and Elisabeth Howard Elliot '48 in recent decades. Or, much earlier, John Wesley Powell, the noted explorer of the American West and pioneering director of the U.S. Geological Survey, who attended classes at the Illinois Institute shortly before this fledgling school was transformed into Wheaton College.

Through the years and through many changes, however, Wheaton has retained its central defining purpose: to serve the church and society through programs of higher education marked by evangelical Christian faith and diligent intellectual effort.

1860–1925

The history of the College can be divided into three fairly distinct phases. First was the era dominated by the long tenures of founding president Jonathan Blanchard (1860-1882) and Blanchard's son Charles (1882-1925). Under the Blanchards, Wheaton's character was fixed as a distinctly evangelical college. When in 1860 the Illinois Institute was reconstituted as Wheaton College, it was only one among many small, locally supported midwestern colleges brought into existence by the westward movement of New Englanders. These New Englanders carried to Illinois and other frontier states their commitment to education as both a Christian and a civilizing enterprise. Jonathan Blanchard's fervent campaigns against Southern slavery, Masonry, and alcohol were, to his friends, noble examples of Christian energy at its best.

But even as Jonathan and then Charles pursued their vision of civilization guided by Christian principles, American society was changing and it was changing fast. The nation's new

research universities, which sprang up after the Civil War, began to separate Christian convictions from academic pursuits and social service. Worried voices in the churches began to ask, if mainstream higher education means practices like the higher criticism of Scripture, do we want any part of it?

Over the last third of the nineteenth century, the common pursuit of educational and social goals within a Protestant evangelical framework became less common. Wheaton, under the Blanchards, stayed about where it had been in 1860. With much of American society and higher education moving on, Wheaton became more distinctive in trying to guide higher education by traditional Christian commitments. In his last decades, Charles Blanchard turned increasingly for support to groups becoming known as fundamentalists, since they were the ones with whom it seemed possible to work at keeping together traditional Christianity, public service, and serious learning.

1925–1965

Wheaton's second transitional phase began after Charles Blanchard died in 1925. During this phase the College had to decide how it would pursue "serious learning" in a distinctly evangelical setting. When J. Oliver Buswell, Jr., was named to replace Blanchard in

1926, he became one of the nation's youngest college presidents. Buswell's tenure was marked by two notable efforts; one of these marked out a path the College would not follow, while the other opened a door to its future. The path not followed was Buswell's identification with conservative and fundamentalist forces in the northern Presbyterian church. College trustees eased Buswell out as president in 1940 when they concluded he was involving the College too closely in the intramural theological battles of his church.

The path that Wheaton did follow was Buswell's effort to improve academic standards. For that purpose, he sought advice from scholars at the University of Chicago and other well-respected national institutions rather than from the network of separatistic fundamentalist colleges that had sprung up earlier in the century. The result was an education increasingly attractive to parents and students from the conservative portions of the American Protestant landscape. During the 1930s, when much of American higher education suffered a steep decline, enrollments at Wheaton steadily increased.

Buswell's successor, V. Raymond Edman (1940-1965), continued on this course. Even as he hustled to accommodate a surge of veterans who had served in World War II, Edman sup-

ported an expanding team of outstanding professors. As scholars, these professors showed how serious learning could build on distinctly Christian foundations. Some of these notables had been hired under Buswell: Russell Mixter '28 in biology (1928-1979), who would offer a discerning Christian assessment of evolution; Clyde Kilby in English (1935-1980), who introduced American evangelicals to C. S. Lewis, J. R. R. Tolkien, and Dorothy L. Sayers; and S. Richey Kamm in history and political science (1940-1973), who pointed students to public life as a form of Christian service. Others in this remarkable generation of professors came on board under Edman: Merrill Tenney (1943-1982), careful, sober, and edifying guide to the Scriptures; Arthur Holmes '50, M.A. '52 (1951-1994), philosopher and teacher extraordinaire; Howard Claassen (1952-1966; 1971-1980), prize-winning research physicist and moving force in founding Wheaton's Human Needs and Global Resources (HNGR) program; Beatrice Batson M.A. '47 (1957-1991), Shakespearean scholar and all-around inspiration. With such eminent scholars pointing the way, Wheaton showed what Christian learning meant in practice as well as precept.

Under President Edman, Wheaton also became closely identified with

the "neo-evangelical" movement that sought to bring traditional Christian faith into fresh, renewed engagement with the world. This movement drew from many sources, but students trained at Wheaton were among the most important. Billy Graham '43, Litt.D. '56 practiced a positive public evangelism. Carl F. H. Henry '38, M.A. '41, Litt.D. '68 became an unusually effective promoter of theological renewal and social engagement as the founding editor of *Christianity Today* magazine. Elisabeth Howard Elliot Gren '48 authored memorable books about the death of her husband Jim Elliot '49 and his missionary colleagues in Ecuador, and later wrote other books as well.

In the period 1940 to 1965, Wheaton remained true to evangelical convictions while beginning to make a difference in broader social, religious, and academic circles. It maintained "fundamentals of the faith" without, for the most part, becoming ingrown, defensive, or sectarian. It is especially noteworthy that the College's remarkable contribution of graduates to missionary service expanded in the very same years that it emerged as a significant intellectual force.

1965–2010

The third phase of Wheaton's history has been defined by the leadership of Hudson Taylor Armerding '41 (1965-1982), J. Richard Chase (1982-1993), and Duane Litfin (1993-2010).

In the face of difficult challenges, a rapidly evolving American culture, and through the crises that educational institutions always face, these presidents have done their best to maintain the founding vision of a distinctly Christian college. They, with administrators and faculty, have expanded on the twin commitments to faith and learning established under Buswell and Edman. The presidents have been asked to raise money, build buildings, maintain high standards, extinguish metaphorical fires, take some heat, and keep the faith. They have overseen faculty and students engaged in learning about more things, with more parts of the world in view, with more searching of Scripture and Christian tradition for answers, and with more evangelical varieties on board.

The College's recent history is too close in its multiple complexity for brief analysis. Yet it is certainly significant that each of Wheaton's recent presidents has both regularly preached in Chapel and worked hard at supporting new faculty as Christian scholars. Although that combination of commitments is now rare in American academic life, it is completely in keeping with Wheaton's heritage.

From its founding to the present, Wheaton College has existed to honor Christ, to promote sound education, to prepare students for service in the world, to aid the church—and to carry out these various goals in reasonable harmony with each other. The effort to pursue such goals together has been neither smooth nor easy. Trustees and presidents; administrators, faculty, and staff; students and their parents; and Wheaton's worldwide constituency of friends and supporters have been pushed by an increasingly secular society that views "Christian learning" as an oxymoron. They have been pulled by forces in evangelical churches that sometimes agree with the secularists, though for opposing reasons.

Progress on the pathway of "Christian learning" has sometimes been rapid; sometimes it has faltered. But it has endured. The main reason is because the College motto, "For Christ and His Kingdom," has functioned as much more than just a motto. It defines three ideals—grateful response to the God who in Christ called out a people for Himself; dedicated action in the world where God through evangelism, discipleship, service, and scholarship is building His kingdom; and faithful efforts to show how such grateful response and such dedicated action can strengthen each other.

Jonathan Blanchard

William Osborne

Adeline Collins

Samuel Stratton

1800s

1860 Wheaton College opens its doors with Jonathan Blanchard as president, welcoming men and women of any race.

1860 The first Wheaton College graduation ceremony is held in Jewell's Grove, about two miles northwest of the College. Seven students receive diplomas: four pastors, two teachers, and one lawyer.

1862 Miss Adeline Collins is the first female graduate and stays to be the dean of ladies, tutoring and training them to handle their hoopskirts, among other things.

1864 Abolitionist Elijah Lovejoy's martyrdom inspires the funding of a scholarship to finance education of African American students, including William Osborne 1876, first Black president of the student Beltionian Society.

1865 At least 298 Wheaton students enlist as Union soldiers at different points throughout the Civil War. Samuel Stratton and Ezra Cook are among them.

When shot in the hand—a wound that eventually became gangrenous—Ezra remained firm in his temperance convictions and refused the shot of whiskey that might have dulled the pain. By the Civil War's end, 26 Wheaton soldiers had died in battle or its aftermath.

1865 The College library, containing 25 volumes, is open from 3:00-5:30 P.M. New book possibilities are voted on by the student literary society. A term fee of 10 cents is charged for use of the library.

A. D. Zaraphonithes

Charles Blanchard

1871 The sky is ablaze with the glow from the Chicago Fire—a glow "so brilliant that [Wheaton] residents could read their newspapers all night for several days without lighting a lamp." Blanchard and students drive supply wagons to the city, sparking a lasting tradition of community service at Wheaton.

1872 Just in time for Christmas tolling, the bell is installed in Blanchard tower.

1873 Two missionaries graduate: A. D. Zaraphonithes serves in Greece, and Henry Martyn Bissel serves in Mexico.

1882 Championing liberal arts education and classical studies, Charles Blanchard succeeds his father as president at only 33 years of age.

1885 A fire breaks out in the hardware store on Front Street. Professors and students join the whole-town effort to stop the spread, hauling water from nearby wells and cisterns.

1890 The "alumni observatory" (a.k.a. the "Lemon") is dedicated on Blanchard's front lawn. The brightly colored dome houses a twelve-and-a-half-inch Newtonian reflecting scope and a seven-inch refracting telescope. In 1972, HoneyRock purchased the observatory for $520, and it was hauled to Wheaton's "northern campus" in Wisconsin.

1894 Pacifist reformer Jane Addams speaks in Chapel five years after founding Hull House in Chicago.

1800s

Coach Harv and Dorothy Chrouser, 1952

1900s

1895 Williston Hall is built in honor of College benefactor J. P. Williston, the inventor of indelible ink, who uses his resources and reputation to help former slaves find freedom and better lives.

1899 Only eight years after the invention of basketball, Wheaton builds a gymnasium featuring a square basketball floor, basement bowling alley, locker rooms, and a second floor running track—32 laps to the mile!

1900 Students take leadership of the school newspaper, *The Record,* which had already been in circulation as a school paper run by the faculty.

1904 The game of basketball makes its first appearance in the Olympics, held in St. Louis, Missouri, as a demonstration sport during the World's Fair. Four different levels of competition are held, and Wheaton College is invited to participate in the college level because they have the best winning percentage of any college in Illinois. The Wheaton team (called by *The Record* the "Wheaton midgets") takes second place.

1909 Donning wigs, a faculty couple dresses in colonial attire to celebrate Washington's birthday at the first "Washington Banquet."

1913 Wheaton's liberal arts curriculum begins to segment into specialized academic departments: Bible, philosophy, social science, and physical science.

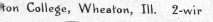

ton College, Wheaton, Ill. 2-wir

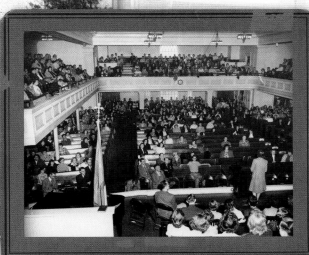

James Oliver Buswell

1915 Wheaton College's preparatory school, Wheaton Academy, receives its own separate faculty and residence in the Industrial Building, later named Schell Hall.

1918 A flurry of khaki sock knitting for soldiers breaks out on campus. Ninety-two Wheaton students are in the U.S. military, and three in the Canadian military. Russell Brooks and Willis Cork are killed in action during WWI.

1921 Distinguished lawyer William Jennings Bryan speaks in Blanchard Hall's Fischer Chapel. According to student Edward Coray '23, Bryan "was a fascinating speaker and spiced his message with some good humor."

1922 Books are signed and photos enjoyed as the first *Tower* yearbook is published.

1923 Mr. Alumni himself (Ed Coray '23) organizes the first Homecoming Weekend, an initiative from the newly appointed student government who promised "a bonfire pep meeting, novel stunts, new yells, songs, speeches, and a band."

1925 Students have long outgrown Fischer Chapel as a meeting place, necessitating the building of Pierce Chapel in cooperation with College Church of Christ.

1926 A non-Blanchard at the helm of Wheaton College? Dr. James Oliver Buswell, Jr. is inaugurated as the youngest college president in the country (at age 31). Under his leadership, the small prairie school bursts into the 20th century.

1900s

1927 Construction on Blanchard is carried on as the east wing is added, and President Buswell sees to it that the building is named for the two Blanchards. The tradition of rubbing J. B.'s nose on the building's bas-relief plaque begins.

1928 On the brink of worldwide economic devastation, President Buswell introduces the "Forward Movement Drive" to secure $1 million for the endowment. The goal is met two months after the stock market collapse that sparks the Great Depression.

1929 The alumni magazine is first published.

1929 Mrs. Helen Spaulding Buswell founds the Faculty Women's Club of Wheaton to extend friendship and service opportunities to staff and faculty women. Besides many activities, such as hosting receptions at Arena Theater and praying weekly for the College, today's Wheaton College Women's Club volunteers manage the Corinthian Co-op, a clothing exchange depot used by staff and students since 1972.

1933 Morning headlines read "ROOSEVELT CLOSES BANKS!" With its bank accounts frozen, the College issues salary vouchers to faculty and accepts IOUs from students who can't access their money to pay tuition. The chapel remains open until midnight all through this tumultuous month. "We have let God take over this campus!" President Buswell declares.

1935 The Wheaton College Science Station in the Black Hills of South Dakota becomes a satellite campus for botany

THE WHEATON RECORD

V. Raymond Edman

*U.S.S. Wheaton in World War II
was named for Wheaton College*

and geology classes under the leadership of professors John W. Leedy and L. Allen Higley.

1935 The first Wheaton soccer team is organized by James McKellin '35, a superintendent of the campus grounds. The team is composed of missionary kids from Scotland, Korea, Iraq, Ireland, China, Japan, India, Canada, and Egypt.

1937 Wheaton College Graduate School opens for students pursuing advanced degrees.

1940 Dr. V. Raymond Edman, a man of courage, integrity, and compassion, is inaugurated as Wheaton's fourth president.

1941 At a time when funding and building materials grow scarce, materials for the Alumni Gymnasium (later Coray Gym) are procured the day before the government puts an embargo on steel, and ground is broken for the new building.

1943 At five o'clock in the afternoon, the Blanchard bell chimes each day until the

end of WWII, as the campus community pauses to remember those in the armed forces.

1945 The *U.S.S. Wheaton Victory* is launched at Terminal Island, California. The *Wheaton* is one in the fleet of victory ships named for America's oldest educational institutions with student bodies over 500.

1947 From the top of Blanchard Hall, WHON (later WETN), the College's radio station, broadcasts College news, sports events, and music.

1900s

1948 "The Christian in Business" is the College's first business conference.

1949 While seniors are on a retreat, juniors from the class of 1950 steal the top of the two-foot-by-seven-foot bench dedicated by the class of 1912 "for seniors only"; this sparks a long-lasting bench rivalry.

1950 For more than 40 consecutive hours, the campus community meets in prayer and repentance, beginning a wave of revival. This is not the first campuswide revival,

nor will it be the last, but it remains a testament to the Holy Spirit's presence in students, faculty, and staff on campus.

1951 Wheaton coach Harvey Chrouser '34, along with his wife Dorothy '34, envision and oversee the founding of HoneyRock, a camp that provides year-round opportunities for training and retreat on 800 acres in the Northwoods of Wisconsin.

1951 In honor of the 39 Wheaton servicemen killed in WWII and

more than 1,600 students who served in the war, the Memorial Student Center is constructed.

1952 Somewhat disputed from its start, Wheaton launches its first ROTC unit, required for all freshmen and sophomore men until 1975 when it becomes voluntary.

1953 Wheaton's first study abroad program travels with Dr. Joseph Free to the Dothan archaeological excavation site. Other programs are later added, including treks

through the Holy Lands, and travels to England, France, Germany, Holland, and East Asia.

1955 Known for being warm-hearted, wise, and accessible, Rev. Evan Welsh '27 becomes Wheaton's first chaplain. He and his wife Olena Mae '41 host Friday night open houses, welcoming all students.

1956 Jim Elliot '49, Ed McCully '49, Nate Saint '50, Roger Youderian, and Pete Fleming lose their lives as missionaries in Ecuador.

1957 Men's basketball makes a slam-dunk, winning Wheaton's first NCAA (College Division) Team Championship.

1958 A group of young men stirred by the passivity toward evangelism on campus meet to discuss what kind of movement could come out of Wheaton, and the Student Missionary Project (SMP) is born.

1961 The science department hosts a symposium on "Origins and Christian Thought," igniting dialogue years before current debates on issues

relating to the integration of faith and science.

1963 More than 1,000 books by and about C. S. Lewis, together with letters and manuscripts, come to English Professor Clyde S. Kilby following the death of Lewis. These mark the beginning of the Marion E. Wade Center that will later house the papers and personal artifacts of J. R. R. Tolkien, Dorothy Sayers, G. K. Chesterton, Owen Barfield, George MacDonald, and Charles Williams.

MACBETH cast performs under new drama policy

Hudson T. Armerding

1900s

1963 The Perry Mastodon is uncovered on the Glen Ellyn property of U.S. Federal District Court Judge Samuel Perry. All 115 pieces of his skeleton are donated to Wheaton College where he stands to greet visitors at the science building.

1965 Dr. Hudson T. Armerding '41 is chosen to be Wheaton's fifth president and Dr. Edman assumes the role of College chancellor. The College's strong emphasis today on the integration of faith and learning crystallizes during the Armerding years.

1965 McAlister Hall opens as the Conservatory of Music. A collection of more than 28,000 music scores, recordings, and reference materials are now housed in Buswell Library.

1966 *Macbeth* is performed on campus under the direction of Professor Edwin Hollatz; this marks the first official staging of a literary drama performed at Wheaton College.

1967 While delivering a Chapel address titled "In the Presence of the King," recounting his visit with the Ethiopian

emperor Haile Selassie, Dr. Edman collapses and enters the presence of the King, Jesus Christ.

1968 Richard Nixon speaks on McCully Field as part of his Republican campaign for the presidency. He urges the crowd, "Strengthen the faith of America. See that young people grow up with faith in God."

1970 Lee Howard '72 returns from a summer spent backpacking in Europe to start Wheaton's Youth Hostel Ministry.

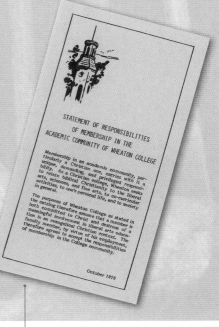

STATEMENT OF RESPONSIBILITIES
OF MEMBERSHIP IN THE
ACADEMIC COMMUNITY OF WHEATON COLLEGE

October 1978

1970 Community School of the Arts (CSA) is founded. Over time, the CSA will annually enroll 1,500 students of all ages to its professional instruction in the fine and performing arts.

1971 Wheaton joins nine other colleges to form the Christian College Consortium.

1971 Illinois Governor Richard Ogilvie delivers the first "Warren L. Wheaton Memorial Address" in Edman Chapel. He expresses grave concern over the "city-type problems" increasingly afflicting the suburbs and calls for imaginative responses for developing better community.

1974 Distressed by reports of famine in Asia, Africa, and South America, professors Howard Claassen and Bee-Lan Wang organize a study/service program called Human Needs and Global Resources (HNGR) with Dr. Wayne Bragg '53, M.A. '57 as the first director.

1979 Wheaton College takes "The Pledge." The Board of Trustees gives assent to the code of conduct officially called the "Statement of Responsibilities of Membership in the Academic Community of Wheaton College."

1980 In 1979 the College begins work on construction of the Billy Graham Center, which is dedicated in September 1980 with Billy '43 and Ruth Bell Graham '43 in attendance. Harold Anderson is not only the general contractor of the Center, but also several other campus buildings.

J. Richard Chase

Duane Litfin

1900s

1982 J. Richard Chase is inaugurated. In his term he offers spiritual guidance and strengthens administrative structures and procedures that attract gifted students who profit from the rigorous academic programs.

1982 "Olé—olé, olé, olé!" Men's soccer wins Wheaton's first NCAA (Div. III) Championship. Women's soccer also wins Div. III championships in 2004, 2006, and 2007.

1984 Vice President George H. W. Bush delivers this year's commencement address.

1986 The $36 million Campaign for Wheaton brings greater endowment and improved facilities. Anderson Commons, the dining hall in part donated by architect and contractor A. Harold Anderson, is built as a result of the campaign.

1987 Gospel Choir becomes an official student organization.

1988 Student Democrats bring Jesse Jackson to campus as part of his campaign for presidency. His rally, held in Pierce Chapel, notes biblical concerns for social justice.

1989 After declining an option to replace the aging Blanchard Hall with a new facility, the Board of Trustees moves to begin renovations to historic Blanchard Hall. Homecoming 1990 includes a celebration of its completion, largely funded by alumni gifts.

1993 Combining pastoral gifts with serious scholarship, Dr. Duane Litfin becomes the new president. He strengthens the faculty and student body, increases the facilities and academic resources of the College, and clarifies its mission and direction.

Stanton L. Jones

_2000s_

1993 Under the leadership of psychology department chairperson Dr. Stanton L. Jones, the Graduate School adds the doctor of psychology program. In 1998 the Psy.D. program receives the seven-year maximum accreditation from the American Psychological Association. In 1996 Dr. Jones is appointed Provost (chief academic officer and second-ranking administrator) of Wheaton College.

1994 Franklin Street is replaced with Chase Commons, a red-brick walking mall lined with flowers, grass, and trees.

1998 Experiential learning grows through the Wheaton in Chicago program, allowing students to study urban issues while interning at organizations and living downtown for a semester.

2000 After cheering for the Wheaton Crusaders since 1927, "Wheaties" root for a new mascot, and the Wheaton Thunder proudly take the field.

2000 The New Century Challenge campaign, under the leadership of Vice President for Advancement Mark Dillon, surpasses its $140 million goal and brings in $157 million, funding the completion of the Sports and Recreation Complex, an updated library, and technological innovations across campus.

2002 Wheaton holds its first official dance in 143 years—a swing dance. Several dozen students crowd the room for free lessons offered the night before.

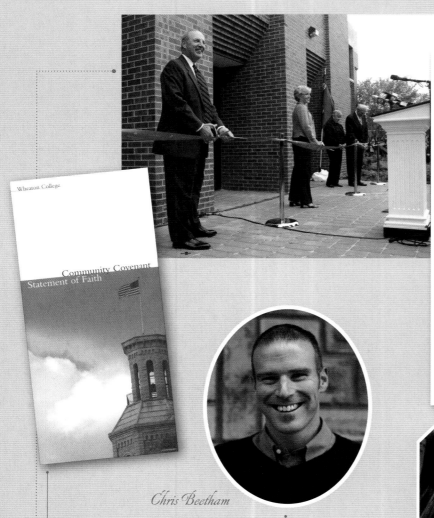

Chris Beetham

2000s

2003 "The Pledge" is replaced by the Community Covenant, a document expressing the biblical convictions the Wheaton community aspires to live by while seeking to fulfill its institutional mission.

2004 The Todd M. Beamer Center is dedicated in the memory of United Flight 93 hero Todd Beamer '91, who died along with Jason Oswald '95, Jeffrey Mladenik M.A. '95, and more than 3,000 others in the terrorist attacks of September 11, 2001.

2005 Wheaton College Graduate School awards its first academic doctoral degree to Chris Beetham '99, Ph.D. '05. Chris takes his Ph.D. in biblical theology to Addis Ababa, Ethiopia, where he becomes a professor at two theological schools.

2006 Student response to help fight global AIDS and extreme poverty prompts President Litfin to sign on to the ONE Campaign. Wheaton becomes the first "College of ONE" in the country.

2007 The $260 million Promise of Wheaton campaign goes public. Besides funding completion of a new math and science building, the Promise campaign will increase student scholarships, foster faculty-student mentoring, strengthen initiatives for evangelism, and expand facilities for the visual and performing arts.

2008 In recognition of the large number of Wheaton graduates in public service, the J. Dennis Hastert Center for Economics, Government and

Philip G. Ryken

Public Policy is dedicated as part of the Promise campaign.

2008 Groundbreaking for a new LEED-certified natural science and mathematics center begins. The new building will feature research labs that open onto teaching labs, a roof made of self-sustaining ground cover, and an interactive atrium museum—the Perry Mastodon's new home.

2009 Adams Hall, home of Wheaton's art department, reopens with a renovated

interior and 11,000 square feet of added space, including two new galleries and a sculpture garden.

2009 The Wheaton Center for Early Christian Studies is founded within the Department of Biblical & Theological Studies. This concentrated program in Patristics and early Christian literature connects the evangelical tradition to its earliest roots.

2010 Students, faculty, and staff convene for the Sesquicentennial Gala—an elegant

event recalling the Washington Banquet in days of old. Hymn-writers Keith and Kristyn Getty announce they are writing a Wheaton hymn inspired by the Sesquicentennial verse, "One generation will commend your works to another; they will tell of your mighty acts" (Psalm 145:4, NIV).

2010 The Board of Trustees announces that Dr. Philip G. Ryken '88 will be the College's eighth president beginning July 1, 2010.

Finding Wheaton and Staying for a Very Long Time

by Dr. Jill Peláez Baumgaertner, Professor of English & Dean of Humanities and Theological Studies

ON A SWELTERING JUNE DAY IN 1980 I FOUND MYSELF SITTING WITH DR. BEATRICE BATSON M.A. '47 IN THE MSC STUPE, sipping a Coke and talking about Shakespeare and John Donne and John Bunyan. I had just finished my dissertation, was looking in the Chicago area for a teaching position, and Beatrice was my guide that afternoon in my introduction to Wheaton College. We had already seen the Perry Mastodon and the Wade Center; and in the English department, on the first floor of Blanchard Hall, I had met Roger Lundin '71, a lanky young man with an intelligent face and a huge smile, who was one of the department's recent hires in nineteenth-century American literature. Sharon Coolidge '72, the newly married department medievalist, also stopped by.

Frustrated as early as 1974 with the secularization of the academy, I had heard about Wheaton College when I was a doctoral student in English at Emory University. My husband and I had been invited to join a weekly Bible study run by Wheaton grads Burt M.A. '54 and Letty Harding, and David and Jane Williams Scott '63. One evening Jane brought me a brochure describing the Writing and Literature Conference at Wheaton on Dorothy Sayers, planned, no doubt, by Dr. Batson. I wondered about a college with "faith and learning" as its mantra. What would education look like in such a place? How in the world would one go about integrating Athens and Jerusalem in the classroom? I had never experienced it myself, and it was intriguing but downright difficult to imagine.

When my husband was transferred to Chicago, no one except for Jane Scott could see any good in the move. I was being wrenched out of my doc-toral program, we had begun to put down permanent roots in Atlanta, our children were happy in school, and we lived reasonably close to family. Jane, however, was convinced that we were being dragged to Chicago so that I could eventually teach at Wheaton. I was not so sure. I still had a disserta-tion to write, a project that could take several years. After our move I plugged away, using the Newberry Library in Chicago as my new research home. In the spring of 1980, when I turned in

the last chapter of the dissertation, I sent off a letter to Dr. Batson, chair of the English department. She called me almost immediately, inviting me to visit Wheaton, and so I found myself that afternoon making my way west from Oak Park, where I lived.

As it turned out, there was no full-time position open in the department at that time, but Beatrice offered me several adjunct courses. This presented me with a dilemma because I had already decided not to accept a part-time position. But Beatrice worked her magic (Frederick Buechner has said that one never says "no" to Dr. Batson!), and I found myself agreeing to teach freshman writing and introductory literature courses.

My intention was to try it out for a while and then find a permanent position elsewhere. My "try-out" period lasted exactly one week, by the end of which I was completely smitten. I had never taught students like these: earnest, smart, funny, thoughtful. They were eager to learn, excited about literature and writing, and then there was that extra ingredient which was so unusual:

they were people of faith and of the Book. Furthermore, these students challenged me to think as I had never thought before—to actually bring my faith into the classroom on a daily basis, to use my faith to expand the meaning of texts, to uncover the meaning of language. I remember to this day the first class devotion I gave, connecting the Word to the written word, the Word made flesh to the incarnational act of poetry. Such freedom in the classroom was exhilarating, I thought at the time, excited by the Wheaton project to link faith and intellect, realizing that "faith seeking understanding" was a concept that originated with Anselm but that had little currency in contemporary academic thought at so many other institutions.

After my first year of adjunct teaching, a permanent, tenure-track position opened. I applied for it and much to my delight found myself in the fall of 1981 a permanent member of the English department. My students during those first years of teaching were particularly memorable because, well, because they were the first: Lori

Ambacher '83, Betty Smartt '87, Carol Miller '85, Kristyn Komarnicki '84, Hope Howell '82, Lisa Swanson '87, Chip Pollard '85, and Jon Carter '86. These were talented writers, careful readers of literature, enthusiastic learners, each of them ready to take the responsibility for their own education. And I—I was constantly challenged by these young minds, so hungry for the language of truth and of Truth. These were among the first students I watched mature from freshmen to seniors, teaching them paragraph structure in Writing 103/104, introducing them to narrative and to poetic image in Imaginative Writing, discussing Shakespeare and George Herbert in majors courses, and helping them learn to live with a certain kind of ambiguity in the complex literatures they read in Senior Seminar.

Then very quickly it seemed, I was awarded promotion and tenure and settled into my life at Wheaton for what has turned out to be the long haul. Teaching was the primary joy, that which gave me energy and helped me gain insight (a teacher learns so much

"We began, in this class, to read Benedetto Croce, Jose Ortega y Gasset, Roger Fry, Herbert Read, Bernard Bosanquet, and I. A. Richard, and we shouted at each other and tore our hair and tried to define beauty and truth and goodness and wrote great splashy papers and looked at paintings and listened to Mozart and wondered if we would ever be able to pull ourselves together. . . . But I felt that once again a door had been blown open and that I could never again insist that there was nothing on the far side."

—THOMAS HOWARD '57, recounting his experience in a class in aesthetics

from her students), that which gave me an adrenalin rush each time I closed the classroom door and walked to the front of the class, that which touched me so frequently with God's grace worked through the combination of the close study of literary texts and the inspiring responses of my students.

But faculty life has other facets, too, and expectations. There are stretches of time during the summer and during sabbaticals when the bustle of students is replaced by intense solitude that is necessary for serious scholarship and writing. What an encouragement it was for me that Wheaton wanted me to be bold, to step outside of my academic specialty to tackle other issues and authors, even occasionally to write poetry rather than scholarly monographs. And whatever I wrote had impact on my teaching because I was a teacher of writers and readers, and I was not asking my students to do anything I had not struggled with myself.

After years of involvement in faculty governance, in the fall of 2001 I became an academic dean at the college that had nurtured me for so many

years. In many ways, there is nothing in the life of a faculty member that prepares one for a very different kind of life in administration, but I firmly believe that an academic dean must be drawn from faculty ranks in order to be effective. As dean of humanities and theological studies I am responsible for recruiting, hiring, nurturing, and reviewing faculty, for advising on curricular issues, for solving problems that arise, and for providing a vision for the future of the division.

My attention has shifted from my students to my faculty, and I must say that they are a most impressive lot. When I arrived on Wheaton's doorstep in 1980, I loved what I encountered, but the environment was different from today. In those days there were few women or faculty of color. Today, while we still face challenges in that area, our demographics have improved considerably. This has worked in a very personal way in my own life. It was a Cuban student who dared me to reclaim my Cuban heritage and who was responsible for my own reemergence as a Peláez. I owe much to this

place that has made me what I am today. It has even made me more Cuban.

We spend much time trying to figure out God's will for us and for our institution. We spend much time trying to resolve tensions that will not disappear. Instead we must take seriously the command to love the Lord our God with all of our heart and all of our strength and all of our mind. We must learn to live and teach those conflicts that create the tensions between religion and higher education. We must engage the secular academic world with mind, body, and spirit. To that end, the Catholic novelist Ron Hansen gives advice, "We try to be formed and held and kept by Christ, but instead he offers us freedom. And now when I try to know his will, his kindness floods me, his great love overwhelms me, and I hear him whisper, Surprise me."

What I have learned at Wheaton is to step out in faith and in humility, aware of imperfections, but also tied to the vision of the kingdom that God has given us in Christ.

"The professors' homes faced the campus, each with its little farm in the rear, on which they and the students more or less practiced athletics, in gaining their meals. President Blanchard's house was located across the railroad, half a mile from the campus. In the summer he usually walked to class, with a heavy cane and stovepipe hat—a hat four sizes larger than any other hat in town. A four-foot plank sidewalk extended from the president's house to the campus, several stretches over watery places. In snowy weather his two-horse bobsled furnished transportation."

—DARIEN STRAW A.L. 1881, M.S. 1884, LITT.D. 1895, remembering Jonathan Blanchard

Dr. Nadine Christine Folino-Rorem
1993-present

Dr. Folino-Rorem is associate professor of marine and invertebrate biology and vice chair of the faculty. Her students collaborate with her as she conducts research on the ecological impact and taxonomy of the invasive hydroid, Cordylophora spp. *Much of her work entails research in the Great Lakes with a focus on the animal in Lake Michigan.*

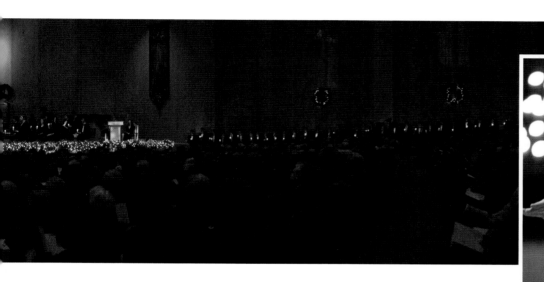

◀ **Dr. Harold M. Best**
1970-1997

A composer of choral and organ works, Dr. Best, professor and dean emeritus of the Conservatory of Music, has authored numerous books on faith and fine arts, worship, and music curriculum. His works include Music Through the Eyes of Faith *(Harper, 1993) and* Unceasing Worship: Biblical Perspectives on Worship and the Arts *(InterVarsity Press, 2003). In addition, he has been active at the national level as a lecturer, consultant, and workshop leader, also serving as president of the National Association of Schools of Music.*

Dr. Daniel Sommerville
1994-present

Dr. Sommerville conducts the Symphony Orchestra and teaches conducting and orchestration. An active guest conductor, music director, and clinician, Dr. Sommerville has also worked with the Metropolitan Youth Symphony Orchestra of Chicago, the Sarajevo Philharmonic, the Northwind Ensemble of Chicago, and in cooperation with conductor John Nelson '63, D.Mus. '89.

Dr. Paul Robinson
1999-present

Before directing Wheaton's Human Needs and Global Resources (HNGR) program, Dr. Robinson spent 40 years living and working in Belgian Congo. His Fulbright scholarship research examined the effects of drought on African communities. Dr. Robinson's current research examines cross-cultural, international, and experiential learning. He continues to work closely with international organizations on development initiatives addressing global challenges of hunger and poverty, including helping to found the Congo Initiative for war-torn Democratic Republic of the Congo.

"How much better to have our witness characterized by the wisdom God has given us, so that it is not our wisdom but the Lord who is glorified. Then people will respond genuinely and lastingly because of the authenticity of what we had to say about Jesus Christ, not because of some clever salesmanship."

—PRESIDENT HUDSON T. ARMERDING '41

Dr. Annette Tomal
1993-present

Department chair and associate professor of business and economics, Dr. Tomal researches gender and religious differences in developing economies, academia, and corporate structure. Her past research has looked at determinants for both abortion and hospital mortality rates. She coauthored Every Parent's Nightmare: How to Find the Best Medical Care for Your Family *(Zondervan, 1993) with her husband, Daniel.*

Dr. Daniel M. Master
2000-present

Dr. Master teaches archaeology and biblical studies at the College and, as part of his research, leads the Leon Levy Expeditions to the ancient city of Ashkelon, situated in southern Israel along the Mediterranean Sea. Through these expeditions, he engages students in one of the most significant American archaeological excavations in Israel.

Dr. John Walford
1981-present

A distinguished art historian and sought-after mentor to students throughout the College, Dr. Walford brings discernment, humor, and humility to his classes. He is currently researching incarnational theology and Renaissance visual culture. "The arts are part of God's provision for our human well-being," he says. "The more these elements are absent from our lives, the more we are alienated from the fullness of life as provided by God."

Dr. Thomas O. Kay
1958-2004

Dr. Kay '53, professor of history emeritus, chaired the department for 15 years. His specializations were ancient Greece, Rome, medieval Europe, and 20th-century Russia. He was active in the community, chairing the DuPage County Housing Authority and serving as vice president of the DuPage County Historical Society.

Senior Teachers of the Year

1960 **ANGELINE JANE BRANDT '27**
Professor of Mathematics, 1936-1968

1961 **KENNETH KANTZER**
Professor of Theology, 1946-1963

1962 **EARLE CAIRNS**
Professor of History, 1943-1977

1963 **E. BEATRICE BATSON M.A. '47**
Professor of English, 1957-1991

1964 **CLYDE KILBY**
Professor of English, 1935-1980

1965 **PHILLIP HOOK**
Assistant Professor of Bible, 1961-1970

1966 **ARTHUR HOLMES '50, M.A. '52**
Professor of Philosophy, 1951-1994

1967 **S. RICHEY KAMM**
Professor of Social Science, 1940-1973

1968 **MERRILL C. TENNEY**
Professor of Bible and Theology, 1943-1982

1969 **RUSSELL MIXTER '28**
Professor of Zoology, 1928-1979

1970 **JOHN LEEDY**
Professor of Botany, 1937-1976

1971 **MORRIS INCH**
Professor of Bible & Theology, 1962-1986

1972 **CYRIL LUCKMAN '37**
Professor of Zoology, 1947-1982

1973 **GORDON FEE**
Associate Professor of Bible, 1969-1974

1974 **JOSEPH LEONARD SPRADLEY**
Professor of Physics, 1959-2007

1975 **BERNARD NELSON '31**
Professor of Chemistry, 1943-1980

1976 **ELLEN R. THOMPSON**
Professor of Music, 1951-1990

1977 **RUSSELL H. PLATZ**
Professor of Music, 1950-1983

1978 **ZONDRA LINDBLADE '55**
Professor of Sociology, 1964-1998

1979 **ALBERT J. SMITH '54**
Professor of Biology, 1967-1999

1980 **GERALD HAWTHORNE '51, M.A. '54**
Professor of Greek, 1953-1995

1981 **GILBERT G. BILEZIKIAN**
*Professor of Biblical Studies, 1966-1968;
1974-1992*

1982 **DEREK A. CHIGNELL M.A. '78**
Professor of Chemistry, 1975-2002

1983 **LELAND RYKEN**
Professor of English, 1968-present

1984 **ARTHUR F. HOLMES '50, M.A. '52**
Professor of Philosophy, 1951-1994

1985 **MARK A. NOLL '68**
Professor of History, 1978-2006

1986 **D. STEPHEN CUSHMAN**
Professor of Music, 1975-1989

1987 **M. JAMES YOUNG**
Professor of Communication, 1972-1995

1988 **MARK R. AMSTUTZ**
Professor of Political Science, 1972-present

*Dr. Gerald Hawthorne
1953-1995*

Spiritual discernment, devotion, and mastery of his subject made Dr. Hawthorne '51, M.A. '54 an outstanding professor of Greek and New Testament studies. Alumni regularly cite him as one of the "most memorable faculty" and in retirement Dr. Hawthorne continues to receive letters of appreciation from former students in ministry around the world.

Mark Lewis
1995-present

After working as an actor in New York for 15 years, Mr. Lewis brought energy, talent, and experience to Arena Theater as its co-director. He is a gifted and respected teacher, sending numerous Wheaton students to premier acting programs and careers in professional theater. He fosters a dynamic community of current and former students around the country, bringing them together for occasional special projects. Mr. Lewis' particular interest is in Shakespearean performance.

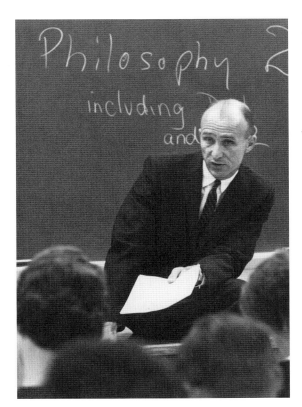

Dr. Arthur F. Holmes
1951-1994

Dr. Holmes '50, M.A. '52 taught philosophy and Bible on Wheaton's faculty, chairing the philosophy department for 37 years. Believing the development of the mind to be a form of praise to the Creator, he wrote The Idea of a Christian College *(Eerdmans, 1987). When asked what steps he took to integrate his Christian faith and academics, Dr. Holmes responded, "Steps? I would rather say this matter has been a* dominant *focus of my professional life."*

Senior Teachers of the Year

1989   LYLE W. DORSETT
Professor of Educational Ministries,
1983-2005

1990   CLIFFORD D. SCHIMMELS
Professor of Education, 1974-1991

1991   JOE H. MCCLATCHEY
Professor of English, 1970-1991

1992   GILBERT G. BILEZIKIAN
Professor of Biblical Studies, 1966-1968;
1974-1992

1993   JAMES JULIUS SCOTT '56
Professor of Biblical Studies, 1977-2000

1994   TERENCE PERCIANTE '67
Professor of Mathematics, 1972-present

1995   ROGER LUNDIN '71
Professor of English, 1978-present

1996   PETER J. HILL
Professor of Business and Economics,
1986-present

1997   E. JOHN WALFORD
Professor of Art, 1981-present

1998   GARY M. BURGE
Professor of New Testament, 1992-present
CHRISTINE GORING KEPNER
Associate Professor of Spanish,
1977-present

1999   LYLE W. DORSETT
Professor of Educational Ministries,
1983-2005
A. SCOTT MOREAU '77
Professor of Intercultural Studies,
1991-present

2000   C. HASSELL BULLOCK
Professor of Old Testament, 1973-2009
GLEN P. TOWN
Professor of Kinesiology, 1981-2003

2001   LYNN COOPER M.A. '74
Associate Professor of Communication,
1978-present
MARY HOPPER '73
Professor of Choral Music and Conducting,
1979-present

2002   JILLIAN LEDERHOUSE '75
Professor of Education, 1979-present
TERENCE H. PERCIANTE '67
Professor of Mathematics, 1972-present

2003   DEAN RAPP '64
Professor of History, 1970-2010
PAUL ROBINSON
Professor of History, Director of HNGR,
1999-present

2004   LISA C. MCMINN
Associate Professor of Sociology,
1998-2006
PETER H. WALTERS
Associate Professor of Applied Health
Science, 1996-present

2005   MARK MCMINN
Professor of Psychology, 1993-2006
H. WAYNE MARTINDALE
Professor of English, 1981-present

Dr. Roger Lundin
1978-present

Dr. Lundin '71, Blanchard
Professor of English, is the
author of many publications
on 19th-century American
literature, hermeneutics, and
the relationship of theology
and literature. He imparts
to his classes an appreciation
for the power of literature,
and the beauty and mystery
of language. He has been a
visiting professor at several
institutions and has received
major research fellowships
from the Erasmus Institute,
the Pew Charitable Trusts,
and the Evangelical Scholarship Initiative.

Dr. E. Beatrice Batson
1957-1991

A student used the words
"majestic," "gracious,"
"authoritative," and "humble"
to describe the mere voice of
Dr. Beatrice Batson M.A.
'47, professor of English
emerita. Taught with dynamic
classroom presence, her scholarship—particularly focused
on Shakespeare—instilled
a love of great literature
in generations of students.
Founder of the Wade
Center's journal, Seven,
she is also coordinator of
Wheaton's Special Collec-
tion on Shakespeare and the
Christian Tradition.

Dr. Helen M. DeVries
1994-2010

Dr. DeVries '65, the director of the doctoral program in psychology, focuses her teaching and scholarly research on life transitions for midlife and older adults. Having written widely in the area of geropsychology, she is in much demand as a speaker. Her compassionate approach to late-life family issues has made her an exceptional mentor to Wheaton's doctoral students, as they serve together at a local community agency.

Dr. Vincent Bacote
2000-present

An associate professor of theology and director of the Center for Applied Christian Ethics, Dr. Bacote urges a Christian worldview that stresses engagement between the church and society, and a faith that impacts every facet of life. His published works include The Spirit in Public Theology: Appropriating the Legacy of Abraham Kuyper *(Baker, 2005).*

Senior Teachers of the Year

2006   ROBERT BRABENEC '60
Professor of Mathematics, 1964-present
L. JONATHAN SAYLOR '81
Professor of Music History and Bassoon, 1989-present

2007   DAVID SETRAN '92, M.A. '94
Associate Professor of Christian Formation & Ministry, 1999-present
CLINTON SHAFFER '84
Associate Professor of German, 1996-present

2008   CAROLYN HART
Associate Professor of Voice, 1999-present
W. JAY WOOD
Professor of Philosophy, 1982-present

2009   KEVIN CARLSON
Associate Professor of Applied Health Science, 2002-present
SCOTTIE MAY '87
Associate Professor of Educational Ministries, 1995-present

Junior Teachers of the Year

1961   WALTER KAISER '55, B.D. '58
Assistant Professor of Bible/Theology, 1958-1966

1962   ROBERT BAPTISTA '44
Professor of Physical Education, 1951-1973

1963   GERALD HAWTHORNE '51, M.A. '54
Professor of Greek, 1953-1995

1964   JAMES KRAAKEVIK '48
Professor of Physics, 1958-1982; Director, Billy Graham Center, 1985-1996

1965   HOWARD CLAASSEN
Professor of Physics, 1952-1966; 1971-1980

1966   WILLIAM DIXON '57
Associate Professor of Chemistry, 1963-1968

1967   ROBERT WARBURTON
Visiting Associate Professor of English, 1958-1968; 1982-1983

1968   MARVIN MAYERS '49
Professor of Anthropology & Linguistics, 1965-1974

1969   MELVIN LORENTZEN '49
Professor of Communication, 1958-1993

1970   ROBERT BRABENEC '60
Professor of Mathematics, 1964-present

1971   ROBERT WEBBER
Professor of Theology, 1968-2000

1972   LELAND RYKEN
Professor of English, 1968-present

1973   LARRY FUNCK
Professor of Chemistry, 1969-present

1974   ALAN F. JOHNSON
Professor of Biblical Studies, 1969-2000

1975   LaVERN BJORKLUND M.A. '63
Professor of Physical Education, 1954-1983

1976   JOE H. McCLATCHEY
Professor of English, 1970-1991

"A sound and thorough education is of priceless value. Yet an education without moral and religious excellence, an enlightened intellect with a corrupt heart, is but a cold gas-light over a sepulcher, revealing, but not warming the dead."

—PRESIDENT JONATHAN BLANCHARD

Dr. Tony L. Payne
1983-present

Director of the Conservatory of Music, Dr. Payne '79 oversees the world-class Artist Series at Wheaton College, 35 full- and part-time faculty, and some 200 music majors. His compositions include music theater works, hymns, and songs for worship. Dr. Payne is a member of the worship commission of the Baptist World Alliance and also serves as minister of music at his local church.

Dr. James Clark
2000-present

A professor of geology, Dr. Clark is interested in hydrogeology and water supply challenges in the developing world. The National Science Foundation and NASA have funded his research on alpine geomorphic processes, climate change, glacial geology, and the Ice Age. Dr. Clark is developing inexpensive geophysical equipment for finding water in developing countries. He and his family served as missionaries in Russia and the scrub jungle of Paraguay.

Dr. Mark Amstutz
1972-present

Dr. Amstutz serves in the politics and international relations department. He travels widely as a teacher, lecturer, and writer. His scholarly focus is on the role of ethics in foreign relations, and his writing centers on international relations, ethics, and political forgiveness. His latest work is International Ethics: Concepts, Theories and Cases in Global Politics *(Rowman & Littlefield, 2008).*

Dr. Jeffrey K. Greenberg
1986-present

Research by professor of geology Jeff Greenberg includes applied geophysics and geochemistry, Precambrian continental development, and the relevance of geoscience to issues in international community development. He has taught 21 different courses at various times, served as department chair, and established the College's environmental science degree program. Dr. Greenberg is interested in the application of earth-science knowledge in missions and community development work.

Junior Teachers of the Year

1977   **TERENCE PERCIANTE '67**
Professor of Mathematics, 1972-present

1978   **EMORY A. GRIFFIN**
Professor of Communication, 1970-2003

1979   **CLIFFORD D. SCHIMMELS**
Professor of Education, 1974-1991

1980   **MARK T. COPPENGER**
Associate Professor of Philosophy, 1975-1981

1981   **SHARON COOLIDGE EWERT '72**
Professor of English, 1977-present

1982   **DOROTHY CHAPPELL**
Professor of Biology, 1977-1994; Dean, Natural and Social Sciences, 2000-present

1983   **DAVID G. BENNER**
Professor of Psychology, 1978-1988

1984   **ROGER W. LUNDIN '71**
Professor of English, 1978-present

1985   **JOHN F. CLARK**
Associate Professor of Spanish, 1964-1995

1986   **BRUCE HOWARD '74**
Professor of Business and Economics, 1980-present

1987   **JAMES PLUEDDEMANN '65, M.A. '71**
Professor of Christian Education, 1980-1993

1988   **KATHLEEN S. KASTNER '71**
Professor of Percussion, 1972-present

1989   **RICHARD E. BUTMAN '73**
Professor of Psychology, 1980-present

1990   **ROBERT YARBROUGH M.A. '82**
Associate Professor of Biblical Studies, 1987-1992

1991   **JEFFREY K. GREENBERG**
Professor of Geology, 1986-present

1992   **DENNIS OKHOLM '74**
Professor of Theology, 1989-2003

1993   **BRIAN MILLER**
Assistant Professor of Chemistry, 1983-1997

1994   **GAIL KIENITZ**
Visiting Assistant Professor of English, 1989-1996

1995   **CYNTHIA NEAL KIMBALL**
Associate Professor of Psychology, 1990-present

1996   **CARLA C. WATERMAN**
Assistant Professor of Educational Ministries, 1993-1998

1997   **DOUGLAS MCCONNELL**
Associate Professor of Missions, 1992-1998

1998   **BRUCE ELLIS BENSON '83**
Professor of Philosophy, 1993-present
NADINE C. FOLINO-ROREM
Associate Professor of Biology, 1993-present

1999   **ANDREA L. BROOMFIELD**
Assistant Professor of English, 1997-2000
MICHAEL LEROY
Associate Professor of Political Science, 1994-2002

Dr. James Plueddemann
1980-1993

Since the age of ten, Jim Plueddemann '65, M.A. '71 wanted to be a missionary; in 1967 he and his wife Carol began serving in Nigeria with SIM. From 1980-1993, Dr. Plueddemann served as dean of Wheaton's Graduate School and as associate professor in Christian education, traveling in summers to Africa, Europe, and South America to assist teachers and administrators of theological schools. Now at Trinity Evangelical Divinity School, he is a Wheaton trustee.

"[The faculty's] ideals and their ability are inestimable in holding Wheaton steadily to its loftiest and worthiest virility. Seniors in service, they continue to give all that they have and are to the best values of Wheaton College."

—The Light Aloft, 1928. This brochure, from the scrapbook of Lucille Swanson '31, highlights the strengths of the College programs and personnel, stating that the campus is "pulsating in tune with Infinite Wisdom."

Dr. Gilbert G. Bilezikian
1966-1968; 1974-1992

A Francophone with an Albanian name, Dr. Bilezikian taught in the Bible department after pastoring in Europe and New York. Former students characterize his classes as "life changing." In addition to his teaching vocation, he was a founding member of Willow Creek Community Church. His many books and articles reflect his expertise as a church planter and a theologian focusing on the church as community.

Dr. Angeline Brandt
1936-1968

Called "a supreme saleswoman for math," Angeline Brandt '27 once said she would "rather teach calculus than eat." Dr. Brandt held a master's degree from Gordon College and a doctorate from the University of Michigan. She was among the first women to be inducted into American Men of Science. In 1960 she received Wheaton's Teacher of the Year award and in 1966, the Distinguished Service to Alma Mater award.

Junior Teachers of the Year

2000   **EVVY HAY CAMPBELL '68**
Associate Professor of Intercultural Studies,
1996-present
JOHN M. MONSON '84
Associate Professor of Archaeology,
1997-2008
ALAN SEAMAN
Associate Professor of Intercultural Studies,
1993-present

2001   **LINDY SCOTT**
Associate Professor of Spanish, 1995-2009
PETER WALHOUT '91
Associate Professor of Chemistry,
1999-present

2002   **CHRISTINA BIEBER LAKE**
Associate Professor of English,
1999-present
MARK LEWIS
Associate Professor of Communication,
1995-present

2003   **JOHN LANE, JR.**
Assistant Professor of Music, 2000-2005
L. KRISTEN PAGE
Associate Professor of Biology,
2000-present

2004   **SARAH BORDEN '95**
Associate Professor of Philosophy,
2001-present
SANDRA FULLERTON JOIREMAN
Professor of Political Science,
2001-present

2005   **LAURA BARWEGEN**
Associate Professor of Education,
2002-present
TIMOTHY LARSEN '89, M.A. '90
Professor of Theology, 2002-present

2006   **WILLIAM STRUTHERS**
Associate Professor of Psychology,
1997-present
DANIEL TREIER
Associate Professor of Theology,
2001-present

2007   **STEPHEN BRETSEN**
Associate Professor of Business and Law,
2003-present
MELISSA FRANKLIN-HARKRIDER
Assistant Professor of History,
2003-present

2008   **CHRISTINE GARDNER**
Assistant Professor of Communication,
2004-present
MICHAEL WESLEY GRAVES '96
Associate Professor of Old Testament,
2004-present

2009   **KELLY FLANAGAN**
Assistant Professor of Psychology,
2005-present
NOAH TOLY '99
Assistant Professor of Political Science,
2006-present

Dr. Henry Allen
1998-present

As a professor of sociology and chair of the department, Dr. Allen '77 not only serves the academy, but also urban churches, social service organizations, school districts, and criminal justice organizations. He employs social scientific research to promote social justice through organizational development, outreach, and policy formation.

James Young
1972-1995

Arena Theater director for more than two decades and the heart and soul of theater at Wheaton, Jim Young created the now well-known Workout group for Wheaton's student actors. His unique approach combined cutting-edge techniques with Christian meaning in a community of actors and directors who learned to interpret human nature and motivation by trusting and loving each other. At his retirement, students returned to campus from 27 states to join in a ceremony honoring Young.

David Hooker
2005-present

Mr. Hooker joined Wheaton's faculty to teach sculpture, ceramics, and art survey. As an artist, his focus is witty ceramic sculptures and the fine arts. As a teacher, curator, exhibition designer, and art school director, his work invites poignant questions about the self and American culture.

Dr. Daniel Burden
2000-present

Associate professor of analytical chemistry, Dr. Burden integrates traditional undergraduate education with interdisciplinary scientific research. As a principal investigator on numerous extramural grants, he has been awarded more than $1.5 million for undergraduate research programs. The most recent grant establishes a new interdisciplinary nanoscale imaging laboratory in Wheaton's new science building. Applications of his work include the biocompatibility of medical implants, molecular understanding of MRSA infections, and the development of new methodologies for nanotechnology.

Senior Scholarship Awards

1998   **SCOTT J. HAFEMANN**
Professor of Greek/Exegesis, 1995-2004
LELAND RYKEN
Professor of English, 1968-present

1999   **DAVID STEWARD BRUCE**
Professor of Biology, 1974-2000
ROBERT C. ROBERTS
Professor of Philosophy/Psychology,
1984-2000

2000   **ALAN R. JACOBS**
Professor of English, 1984-present
JOEL SHEESLEY '72
Professor of Art, 1974-present

2001   **DEAN ARNOLD '64**
Professor of Anthropology, 1973-present
ROBERT GREGORY
Professor of Psychology, 1995-present

2002   **MARK NOLL '68**
Professor of History, 1978-2006
E. JOHN WALFORD
Professor of Art, 1981-present

2003   **JAMES CLARK**
Professor of Geology, 2000-present
P. J. HILL
Professor of Business and Economics,
1986-present

2004   **KENT GRAMM**
Professor of English, 1988-2008
JAMES C. WILHOIT
Professor of Christian Formation & Ministry,
1981-present

2005   **MARK AMSTUTZ**
Professor of Political Science, 1972-present
JOHN WALTON M.A. '75
Professor of Old Testament, 2001-present

2006   **BRUCE ELLIS BENSON '83**
Professor of Philosophy, 1993-present
HELEN M. DE VRIES '65
Professor of Psychology, 1994-2010

2007   **ANDREW HILL**
Professor of Old Testament, 1984-present
FRED VAN DYKE
Professor of Biology, 2001-present

2008   **ANDREW BRULLE**
Professor of Education, 1997-present
GENE GREEN '76, M.A. '77
Professor of New Testament, 1996-present

2009   **DANIEL HORN**
Professor of Piano, 1984-present
DANIEL MASTER
Associate Professor of Archaeology,
2000-present

Dr. Walter Elwell
1975-2004

When Dr. Walter Elwell '59, M.A. '61 received applause at the end of a particularly inspiring Bible course, he responded, "Go and do thou likewise." A prolific scholar with an encyclopedic memory, Dr. Elwell authored or edited more than 40 Bible commentaries, dictionaries, handbooks, encyclopedias, and New Testament studies, including the Evangelical Dictionary of Theology, *chosen by* Christianity Today *as Book of the Year for 1985. Dr. Elwell also edited the two-volume* Baker Encyclopedia of the Bible, *the only evangelical reference book allowed in China in the years immediately following the Tiananmen Square incident. Dr. Elwell was also instrumental in pioneering the annual summer studies program for Eastern European church leaders.*

*◄ **Dr. Mark Niemczyk***
1975-present

Studying the process of photosynthesis, professor of organic chemistry Dr. Mark Niemczyk and a team of researchers at Argonne National Laboratory discovered the key to making charge separation of ion pairs efficient and long-lived in the solid state—creating, in effect, "molecular batteries." In addition to his work at Argonne, Dr. Niemczyk has conducted research at Northwestern University and the University of Chicago.

"In terms of the commitment of the faculty and the students, Wheaton is a model that I hold up as an ideal. . . . I learned what quality collegiate education is at Wheaton. There you have faculty who are deeply interested in learning, but also deeply interested in students."

—Dr. Nathan O. Hatch '68

Julia Blanchard
1908-1948

Julia Eleanor Blanchard 1899, M.A. 1904, LITT.D. '48, the daughter of Charles Blanchard and granddaughter of Jonathan and Mary Blanchard, earned her M.A. in library science from the University of Illinois. Affectionately known as "Miss Julia," she served as the College's librarian for 40 years, single-handedly expanding the book collection by thousands of volumes and serving as the first College archivist.

Mignon Bollman MacKenzie
1928-1967

Mrs. MacKenzie '33, called "Mrs. Mac" by students, left a career as a lyric soprano to join Wheaton's faculty. During her first five years, she earned her bachelor's degree in music along with her students. She taught voice and directed the Women's Glee Club. She instructed the young women to wear dress shoes, hats, and gloves, insisting that "every performance is a witness and must be the best." She was the first recipient of Wheaton College Alumni Association's Alumna of the Year award.

"I undertake to give my students everything that is in me because I think the teacher is the only man in the world who can give himself away and still have more than when he started. I learn much from my students. Every freshman class has brought me new viewpoints."

—DR. DARIEN STRAW A.L. 1881, M.S. 1884, LITT.D. 1895, professor of rhetoric and logic, who served the College for more than 58 years

Dr. Joseph Free
1934-1966

Educator, archaeologist, author, and speaker, Dr. Free served as chair of the archaeology and Bible department from 1943 to 1966. He led nine Wheaton excavations to Dothan in the northern Samarian hills of Israel. Aided by his wife Ruby and students, he uncovered an important city of ancient Palestine, yielding a rich store of biblical artifacts. His book Archeology and Bible History *(Zondervan, 1950) continues to be in print.*

Dr. Lyle W. Dorsett
1983-2005

Dr. Dorsett began his tenure at Wheaton as the second curator of the Marion E. Wade Center, and taught courses in Christian thought, urban American history, and evangelism. His popularity grew so much that one spring one of his courses reached capacity before registration even began. He is the author of And God Came In *(Hendrickson, 2009).*

Clayton E. Halvorsen
1957-1988

Mr. Halvorsen, professor of
music emeritus, directed the
Men's Glee Club for three
decades. He initiated the
European tours, in which the
Club sang in Notre Dame,
Paris; St. Paul's, London; St.
Thomas' Church, Leipzig;
and the presentation concert
for her Majesty Queen
Juliana of Holland. In 1979
and 1983 the Club won
first prize in the male chorus
division at the Interna-
tional Music Festival in The
Hague. A mentor to countless
students, he is remembered for
his rich, baritone solo voice
and gentlemanly direction of
numerous choral groups.

Dr. Dorothy F. Chappell
1977-1994; 2000-present

As a professor of biology, Dr. Chappell explored the biochemistry and ultrastructure of green algae. She now serves as dean
of natural and social sciences and has been a driving force in
bringing the College's new Science Center to fulfillment. In
1981 she was described as "thorough in scholarship; demanding
of excellence, yet sensitive to the learning process; modest and
kind, yet firm in convictions and opinions."

Dr. Paul M. Wright
1929-1970

In his 41 years at Wheaton, "Doc" Wright '26 possessed creativity and foresight that ranged far beyond his role as professor and chair of the chemistry department. He served on the United States Atomic Energy Commission and as a research associate and consultant for Argonne National Laboratory. He helped establish the Wheaton College Science Station in the Black Hills of South Dakota, and as a licensed pilot, assisted in developing the first twin-engine missionary plane.

Dr. J. Derek McNeil
1996-present

Dr. McNeil's varied research experience and interests include ethnic and racial socialization, the role of forgiveness in peace-making, marital disillusionment and resilience, and the integration of psychology and theology. Associate professor in the Graduate School's psychology department, he has written chapters in Why Psychology Needs Theology *(Eerdmans, 2005),* This Side of Heaven: Race, Ethnicity and Christian Faith *(Oxford, 2007),* A Credible Witness: Reflections on Power, Evangelism and Race *(IVP, 2008), and* Integrating Faith and Psychology *(IVP, 2010).*

"To the educational world we pledge our continued commitment to rigorous scholarship and academic excellence. We welcome the opportunity to measure up to the exacting standards which membership in the academic community demands."

—President J. Richard Chase

Dr. Timothy Larsen
2002-present

Dr. Larsen '89, M.A. '90 joined Wheaton's faculty in 2002 as the McManis Professor of Christian Thought. His intellectual interests include areas of British history, historical theology, Christian thought, and intellectual currents and controversies. The periodical Books & Culture *named his book* Crisis of Doubt: Honest Faith in Nineteenth-Century England *(Oxford, 2006) the 2006 Book of the Year.*

Dr. Robert Webber
1968-2000

A theologian of ancient and future faith, Dr. Webber was a gifted teacher whose humor and creativity in the classroom endeared him to generations of Wheaton students. A prolific writer, his some 40 books on the topic of worship were highly influential in demonstrating how the practices of the early church have value for 21st-century Christianity. Dr. Webber founded the Institute for Worship Studies in Jacksonville, Florida, in 1993.

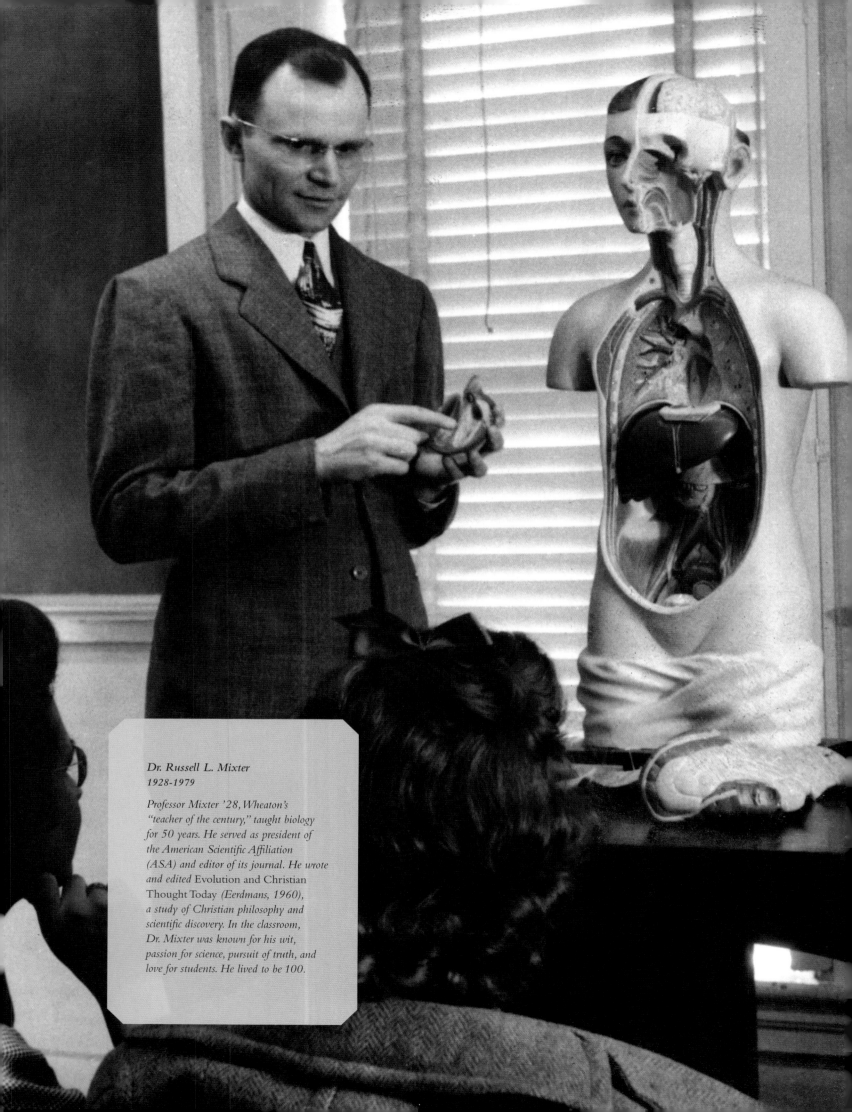

Dr. Russell L. Mixter
1928-1979

*Professor Mixter '28, Wheaton's
"teacher of the century," taught biology
for 50 years. He served as president of
the American Scientific Affiliation
(ASA) and editor of its journal. He wrote
and edited* Evolution and Christian
Thought Today *(Eerdmans, 1960),
a study of Christian philosophy and
scientific discovery. In the classroom,
Dr. Mixter was known for his wit,
passion for science, pursuit of truth, and
love for students. He lived to be 100.*

"Pretend that you've got a book in either hand. One is a great novel, and the other, a textbook. Now throw both up into the air. The text will fall to the ground—and probably break—but the novel will keep right on going, up and up. And if you're smart, you will tie a lasso around it, and let it take you away."

—English Professor DR. JOSEPH H. McCLATCHEY

Dr. Peter J. Hill
1986-present

Occupying the George F. Bennett Chair in Economics, Dr. Hill is an authority in economic history, principles of property rights and institutional change, and comparative economic systems. He is involved in writing, teaching, research, and other professional activities. He serves on a team of American economists offering guidance to the Bulgarian government on privatizing the economy.

Dr. Jill Peláez Baumgaertner
1980-present

Professor of English before becoming dean of humanities and theological studies in 2001, Dr. Baumgaertner specializes in 17th-century British Renaissance literature and creative writing. An award-winning poet, she has authored one volume of collected poems, three chapbooks, a poetry anthology, and a textbook on the writings of Flannery O'Connor.

Joel Sheesley
1974-present

Mr. Sheesley '72 explores the world of art with his students, teaching them how to paint, draw, execute etchings and lithographs, and to engage in the contemporary art world. An active artist and exhibitor of his own work, Mr. Sheesley's body of paintings attests to the intensity of his inner journey. Of Wheaton's art department he says, *"Our involvement with art is a calling through which we play a part in making God's kingdom manifest."*

Dr. Stuart C. Hackett
1963-1978

Known for his eccentric teaching style, Dr. Hackett M.A. '47 taught philosophy at Wheaton. His love for his subject matter and his students was evident when he taught a class. He once said, "I pray to God before my classes that if I speak what is untrue, my students would not remember it, and if what I say is true, they would never forget it." He is the author of three books.

Dr. Kenneth R. Chase
1994-present

Dr. Chase serves as chair and associate professor of communication; he was also the director of the Center for Applied Christian Ethics for seven years. He teaches public speaking, rhetorical theory, and communication ethics. His work has been published in numerous journals, and he co-edited Must Christianity Be Violent? Reflections on History, Practice, and Theology *(Brazos, 2003).*

Dr. Johann S. Buis
2003-present

*Educated across three continents, Dr. Buis
came to Wheaton as an associate professor
of music history. A Fulbright Scholar and
Rockefeller Resident Research Fellow,
he combines studies in music composition
and theory with anthropology, sociology,
and history, telling stories from his native
South Africa along with his lessons. He has
lectured for the Chicago Symphony Orchestra, the Civic Orchestra of Chicago, and the
Art Institute of Chicago.*

Dr. Bruce Howard
1980-present

*Dr. Howard '74, professor of business and economics, currently researches the
impact of interest rates on consumer behavior. He is the author of* Safe & Sound,
Why You Can Stand Secure on the Future of the United States Economy
(Tyndale, 1996) and You Can't Spank a Kid in a Snowsuit *(Tyndale, 1994).*

"I have been deeply blessed and irrevocably formed as a Christian as much through what my professors understood about me and how they responded to that understanding, as by what they taught me. In fact, I would consider anything less to be a rather hollow educational experience. To all of you who taught me, both in the classroom and in the world, bless you and thank you."

—NANCE WABSHAW '73

Dr. Sandra Fullerton Joireman
2001-present

A Fulbright scholarship enabled Dr. Joireman, professor of politics and international relations, to travel the African continent, researching for her first book: Property Rights and Political Development in Ethiopia and Eritrea *(James Currey, 2000). "One of my goals," she says, "is to help educate a generation of Christians who can contribute to development around the world in a thoughtful, productive way."*

Faculty who taught in the Graduate School, circa early 1950s

Seated, l to r: Carl Armerding, Lois LeBar M.A. '45, Mary LeBar M.A. '45, Rebecca Price LL.D. '56, Merrill Tenney. Standing: John Luchies, Berkeley Mickelsen '42, M.A. '45, B.D. '48, Samuel Schultz, Steven Barabas, Kenneth Kantzer L.H.D. '88, Earle Cairns, Eugene Harrison, Frank Neuberg.

Dr. Edwin A. Hollatz
1955-2003

Dr. Hollatz G.S. '55, speech professor at Wheaton, had two goals for speech communication at the College: a credible, licensed radio station, and a drama program with a valid curriculum. Both became reality. His production of Macbeth in 1966 was the College's first official staging of a major play.

Dr. Larry Funck
1969-present

Dr. Funck has served as department chair in addition to teaching general chemistry, inorganic chemistry, and theories of origins. In 2009 he was appointed the chief reader for the College Board's Advanced Placement Chemistry Program, and serves as a consultant for that body. In 1995-96, as a Fulbright scholar, he taught at the University of Lesotho.

Dr. David Bruce
1974-2000

Dr. Bruce, professor of physiology, researched the biochemistry of hibernation, anticipating a day when hibernation research would be used as an anesthetic agent, or to put a tumor into suspended animation. He welcomed students into his research long before such collaboration was considered key to developing new scientists.

Dr. Stephen Moshier
1991-present

Chair of the geology and environmental science department, Dr. Moshier has practiced geology as an academic and as an oil company explorationist. His recent research is in the field of geoarchaeology. During academic breaks he is a team geologist at the excavation of Tell el-Borg, an ancient Egyptian New Kingdom site near the Suez Canal. Dr. Moshier involves his students with fieldwork in Egypt, and during semesters at Wheaton, with lab and remote-sensing work.

Dr. Amy Black
2001-present

Prior to coming to Wheaton, Dr. Black, associate professor of politics and international relations, worked on Capitol Hill as an American Political Science Association Congressional Fellow. This provided the idea for her book From Inspiration to Legislation: How an Idea Becomes a Bill *(Prentice Hall, 2006). Her latest book,* Beyond Left and Right: Helping Christians Make Sense of American Politics *(Baker, 2008), approaches politics as a means of demonstrating Christian love in action.*

Dr. Sharon Coolidge—1977-present and Dr. Norman J. Ewert—1973-present

English department chair, Dr. Coolidge '72, and her husband, business and economic professor Dr. Ewert, have extended open invitations for dinner and conversation at their home every Thursday evening during the past 30 academic years. On average, 40 students attend. Dr. Coolidge's scholarly research includes medieval literature, theology, and art. Dr. Ewert teaches macro-economics, economic growth and development, and small-scale enterprise. Both are actively involved in peace and justice issues.

Dr. Clarence Hale
1928-1974

Dr. Hale '28 remained at his alma mater to teach foreign language, focusing on Greek. He chaired the foreign language department for 19 years and authored two books— Let's Study Greek *and* Let's Read Greek. *The 1951* Tower *yearbook dedicated in his honor read: "For 22 years, his language classes at Wheaton have laughed their way through the limitless Hale repertoire of classroom capers."*

Dr. William Phemister
1972-2007

Dr. Phemister, professor of piano, has led workshops and performed on five continents. Winner of a Fulbright grant and a published composer, he continues to compose, edit, transcribe, and record many piano compositions. He enjoys teaching students to think creatively and energetically about their faith—he himself often spends weekends giving concerts and workshops for inmates in prison.

Dr. John Gration
1975-1994

After spending time as a missionary to Belgian Congo (now Democratic Republic of the Congo) and later Kenya, Dr. Gration M.A. '52 returned to Wheaton in 1975 to join the graduate missions program. In 1985 he became chair of the new missions/intercultural studies graduate program.

Dr. Wilbert Norton
1965-1980; 1983-1987

International missionary statesman, professor, and administrator, Dr. Norton '36 spent a decade in Belgian Congo (now Democratic Republic of the Congo), where he founded Goyongo Theological Seminary. He lectured in seminaries in Croatia, Sweden, the Central African Republic, and Australia before becoming professor of missions and evangelism and dean of the Wheaton College Graduate School. Dr. Norton established and served as principal of the Jos Theological Seminary in Nigeria in 1980 and returned to Wheaton as chaplain for international graduate students.

Dr. Elsie Storrs Dow
1889-1942

Dr. Dow 1881, M.A. 1884 returned as professor of English to her alma mater in 1889 and dedicated more than half a century to educating Wheaton students. Wheaton faculty published a small book of her poems in recognition of meritorious service, stating that "her intellect was capacious, her sympathies wide; her own expression varied and beautiful." When Dow died in 1944, two years after her retirement, the American flag on Blanchard's tower was lowered to half-staff.

Dr. Darien A. Straw
1882-1940

In his 58 years at Wheaton, the multitalented Dr. Straw A.L. 1881, M.S. 1884, Litt.D. 1895 was first secretary then principal of the Academy, joining the College faculty in 1909. He taught logic, rhetoric, sociology, political science, and philosophy. He was a gifted administrator, becoming chair of the history department. When he was a student, he studied and slept in a room in Blanchard Hall that was used as the treasurer's office during the day.

Dr. Mark A. Noll
1978-2006

Dr. Noll '68, McManis Professor of Christian Thought, taught history and theology. With Professor Edith Blumhofer, he cofounded the Institute for the Study of American Evangelicals. In 2005 Time *magazine named Dr. Noll one of the 25 most influential evangelicals in America. While at Wheaton, he published 16 books, including* The Scandal of the Evangelical Mind *(Eerdmans, 1995), and became a leading scholar in the narrative of American religious history and evangelicalism.*

Dr. Douglas J. Moo
2000-present

From the time of Dr. Moo's conversion to Christianity as a senior in college, he has devoted himself to understanding the text of the Bible. His academic interests revolve around the interface of exegesis and theology, focusing on Pauline theology and epistles, most recently, Romans. The Blanchard Professor of New Testament, Dr. Moo has written or co-written several commentaries, and numerous articles and books. He serves on the Committee on Bible Translation, a group of scholars revising the text of the New International Version.

Dr. Terence Perciante
1972-present

Dr. Perciante '67 chairs the mathematics and computer science department, as well as contributing to frequent keynote addresses at National Science Foundation symposia. Dr. Perciante has worked on fractal geometry and chaos theory with an international team of researchers at the University of Bremen. He has authored numerous educational software packages and recently completed an electronic course on historical patterns in fractal geometry.

Dr. Paul Wiens
1981-present

Dr. Wiens teaches choral music and conducting in Wheaton's Conservatory of Music and directs the Concert Choir. He served as Chorus Master for four Artist Series performances conducted by maestro John Nelson '63, D.Mus. '89 and again as Chorus Master for the Wheaton College 150th Anniversary performance of the Brahms Requiem. He authored Expressive Conducting (Self, 2005), a multimedia resource that teaches conducting.

Seeing the Invisible at Work

by Dr. Samuel A. Shellhamer, Vice President for Student Development, retired

WHEN I CAME TO WHEATON COLLEGE IN 1978, my primary focus was to discern how the Lord might use me to serve students. Instead, and in countless ways, students have enriched my life and pointed me to the person of Jesus Christ.

The mission of Student Development at Wheaton is "Touching of Life to Life." Our work is about relationships, and over the years my colleagues and I have been struck by the many different ways Christ has used us in our relationships with students. We have also come to realize that in the process, He has shaped, directed, and enriched our own lives as well.

Following are five significant ways I have seen evidence of God at work.

In Prayer
"Devote yourselves to prayer, being watchful and thankful." Colossians 4:2 (NIV)

The first year I was at Wheaton, a group of freshmen invited me to attend a prayer meeting every Thursday morning at 7:30 in Fischer Hall. This self-initiated devotion to prayer humbled and inspired me, and together these students and I experienced our first year at Wheaton by praying for one another.

In the 29 years that followed during my tenure in Student Development, these prayer times continued, as nine or ten students and I met to pray for the needs of our campus and our own personal concerns. Prayer logs recorded the ways God answered.

The themes of these prayers often revolved around relationships—whether with parents, roommates, friends, or significant others. And through these weekly meetings, I've had the privilege of watching God's redemptive, restorative grace at work, as students who had been making poor choices grew in wisdom. This year-in-and-year-out focus also led me to study more about prayer, discovering books such as John Baillie's *Daily Diary of Prayers* and Richard Foster's *A Celebration of Discipline.*

Over the years, it has been inspiring to see how learning to submit everything to the Lord in prayer, and then experiencing His response, became important to students—especially to those who began meeting with me after getting into some sort of trouble.

In Sorrow
"Mourn with those who mourn."
Romans 12:15b (NIV)

Suffering has brought the lives of our students, and some parents, closest to my own. One year early in the fall semester, I had to call a new freshman student out of class and inform him that his father had just been killed in an auto accident. Dealing together with such a devastating experience brought about a long-term relationship. This student would in time serve as a resident assistant and after graduating, pursue a career caring for college students himself, as a dean of students.

Several years later, I found my life touched again, this time by two parents who had just lost their son—a Wheaton student—in a tragic van accident. I have kept in touch with

Generation after generation—students having the time of their lives

"It was the students who made Wheaton. It is their youth, their intelligence, their vigor, their alertness, the potential power for good which they represent."

—MARGARET MORTENSON LANDON '25 *in an article in* Wheaton Alumni News, *January 1938*

this couple since the accident in 1994, and have been amazed at the depth of their faith and the strength of their relationships with Christ. There was a lack of anger, and a real sense of grace and acceptance in the midst of their grief.

The evidence of Christ in the lives of these and others has helped me not only counsel and comfort students, but also kept me centered on Him when I experienced the loss of my own father, mother, and a younger brother.

In Justice
"He has showed you, O man, what is good. And what does the Lord require of you? To act justly and to love mercy and to walk humbly with your God." Micah 6:8 (NIV)

A very different kind of human suffering eluded me in my early years at Wheaton. Then in February 1992, three African American students walked into my office. They had been refused service in a local business establishment.

I decided to go with them to confront the owner of the business.

As a result of this meeting, I began to see more clearly the prevalence of racism and my own lack of understanding about the issues of racism in our culture. This incident became the source of my passion for being a more careful listener; for actively seeking relationships with students of color; and for supporting the Gospel Choir, the urban studies program, and diversity initiatives on campus.

It's my hope that Wheaton will continue to be a campus that fully reflects and celebrates the diversity within the body of Christ.

In Service
"Be shepherds of God's flock that is under your care, serving as overseers—not because you must, but because you are willing, as God wants you to be; not greedy for money, but eager to serve; not lording it over those entrusted to you, but being examples to the flock." 1 Peter 5:2-3 (NIV)

One of the greatest privileges of working in Student Development has been the opportunity to serve

alongside students, visiting and working with churches and missions around the globe.

The year after I arrived at Wheaton, Jack Swartz '52, a longtime coach and athletic director, and I accompanied 60 students to the Dominican Republic to build temporary housing for families who lost their homes in the wake of Hurricane David. It was my first exposure to a third-world setting.

This was only the beginning of cross-cultural experiences. Since that time, I have traveled to Honduras with students to build a water system for a rural village; to the jungles of what was then Irian Jaya; the streets of India; and the city dumps of Manila, Philippines—all to visit students serving with the Student Missionary Project. I have walked the streets of Chicago on a Friday night with alumnus John Green '87, who founded Emmaus Ministries, an outreach that ministers to male prostitutes in Chicago. I have also traveled to Latvia with Paul Minakov,

a carpenter with the College's physical plant who was imprisoned for two and a half years for his faith in Russia. He has since started Hope International Ministries, which sponsors summer camps for kids at risk. I was a camp counselor to a group of eight boys, most of whom had been orphaned or discarded.

Through many of these experiences, I've watched as the lives of very different people touched and dramatically changed the lives of Wheaton's students, and my own life as well. What consistently impressed me throughout most of my travels was the preeminence of Christ in the lives of His people, especially in disadvantaged communities. Coming home, I have found that it is always more of a struggle to keep Christ at the center, as it is easy to get caught up in our comforts. What helps, I find, is continued involvement with missions. Helping people such as John and Paul grow their ministries is a work I hope to continue for many years.

In Grace

"God is able to make all grace abound to you, so that in all things at all times, having all that you need, you will abound in every good work." 2 Corinthians 9:8 (NIV)

Reflecting on my 30 years at Wheaton College, I realize how much my life has been enriched through relationships. Serving under the leadership of the Board of Trustees and three presidents has been a privilege. Working with fellow Student Development staff members and coaches has been a joy. Meeting weekly for 29 years with a group of men from our faculty and staff has provided a source of continuity and encouragement. But the greatest enrichment has come from investing in the lives of students.

Even though I'm now retired, I hear from Wheaton alumni who are building and serving His kingdom around the globe. Just in the last week, I had a phone call from a graduate who is working in a government position in the state of Indiana. I received a letter from a former student

who is a physician in an inner-city setting providing medical care for the underserved. I met with an alumnus who has returned from Japan after serving there as a missionary for two and a half years. I received an email from a missionary in Costa Rica for whom my wife and I provided premarital counseling 15 years ago. I attended a fundraiser for a ministry in Chicago that was founded in the late eighties by a Wheaton graduate. I had lunch with a couple in Chicago who are serving as foster parents for three children. I received an email from a soldier serving in Iraq.

The Lord has been faithful over the past 150 years to faculty, staff, administrators, and students who have sought to fulfill the mission of Wheaton College. Christ will continue to make grace abound in those who lead the College in the future, as they follow the admonition in Hebrews 10:23 (NIV): "Let us hold unswervingly to the hope we profess, for he who promised is faithful."

Up through the 1930s, nearly 95 percent of the Wheaton College student body belonged to one of "the Lits"—student literary societies providing a social outlet as well as experience in debate, oratory, and parliamentary practice.

Ask any person acquainted with Wheaton College to describe the typical Wheaton student, and you'll likely hear this word: intense. From Lit Society parliaments, to athletic competitions, to life's imponderable questions posted on the Forum Wall, students at Wheaton College have inherited Jonathan Blanchard's earnestness to channel faith and learning into the creative energy of the campus and the complex needs of the world.

Among the men's literary societies, the Beltionians inclined toward theology and the Excelsiors, sports. In the days before a Student Activities Office existed, the Lits offered a place where lasting friendships formed between Wheaton students. Inter-society activities between groups included joint chapels, debating, picnics, parties, and formal banquets.

Beltionian Literary Society
Wheaton College 1891

BELTIONIAN
senior · Program

BELT HALL   JUNE 1, '23

~ Roll Call ~
Scripture and Prayer
Music ---- Blasius
Extempore
Lecture ---- Harris
Reading ---- Cox
Music ---- Blasius
Impromptus
Critique -- E. Coray
Parliamentary Drill -- King
Remarks -- E. Dyrness

From the scrapbook of freshman Martha Dunham Schingoethe '41

one of rambling roses
Paul Bennehoff brought
me in June 1938.

Each literary society conveyed a unique personality—especially the women's groups. The Aelioians and Philatheans were seen as the more scholarly societies, the Boethallians more socially minded, and the Ladosians, athletic.

Boethallian
Literary
Society

•

ANNUAL INFORMAL
OCTOBER 14, 1938

Preface

Once upon a time—
There Was
A Fairy Princess
Held Captive
In a Gruesome Grotto
Until One Day
Her Hero Came,
Broke the Spell
And Set Her Free.

The Aelioians
1894-95

The 1930 "Bows" at Homecoming

"*At 8:45 Friday nite, September 15, 1939,* the Big 4 whistled out of Eldorado carrying with it a strangely happy 17 yr. old girl 'en route' to college. By 7:00 the following morning she was deeply engrossed with the multitude of fascinations Chicago always has in store. At the end of the way, there she was all alone! But not for long because here came Mr. and Mrs. Dahlin to welcome her. Leaving the LaSalle Street Station, a delightful ride ensued, via Oak Park, where we three feasted hungrily on waffles and bacon, etc. Then . . . on to Wheaton . . . how exciting to a frosh who has never before seen her campus! I'm really here; my dream is realized. . . . Praise God—He answers prayer!"*

—From the scrapbook of
CHARLOTTE MEREDITH BROWN HARTZELL '43

Excelsior parliament meeting in 1921

In 1910 President Charles Blanchard remarked that the "religious prosperity" of the College was largely because fraternities had never been allowed. Instead, "acquaintance with literature, acquaintance with art, acquaintance with science, anything which rests the mind, strengthens the body, purifies the heart, ennobles the life is favored . . . and aided by the institution."

1924 literary society

We'll look for you at the Baby Bow Breakfast Friday – Feb. 16 – 7 A.M. – 15¢ Lower Chapel
R.S.V.P. – Must be in to V. Chamberlain by Wed. – Please give Dinning Hall

from the scrapbook of Esther Lou Young DePue '42

1925 Student Volunteer Movement. *Fifty-five graduates committed themselves to missionary service from 1920-1925, traveling to China, the Congo, and the tip of South America. The number is striking considering the average class size was forty-nine.*

By the mid-1900s, Wheaton students' worldviews had been challenged by two world wars. Overseas missions, previously mobilized by denominations, were gaining momentum through the participation of student volunteers. "The evangelization of the world in this generation" became the watchword of the national Student Volunteer Movement that flourished on Wheaton's campus.

As Human Needs and Global Resources interns live in communities torn apart by war, poverty, or apartheid, they learn to look for truth in the midst of tragedy. They discover that service is not an action, but a relationship they will cherish for the rest of their lives.

Since 1976, students enrolled in Wheaton's Human Needs and Global Resources (HNGR) program have combined field-based service-learning internships with transformational initiatives that help people in the Global South live whole, secure, and productive lives.

In October 1871 President Jonathan Blanchard, professors, and students responded to the devastation of the Great Chicago Fire by driving wagonloads of food into the charred remains of the city. In 2005 the campus responded similarly to wreckage wrought on the Gulf Coast by Hurricanes Rita and Katrina. More than 150 faculty, staff, and students spent their Thanksgiving vacation working with teams in Louisiana to restore devastated homes.

Since 1970 more than 600 Wheaton students have spent their summers backpacking across Europe with YHM. Youth Hostel Ministry, sponsored through the Office of Christian Outreach, places Wheaton students in the path of fellow European youth who have taken questions about faith and the meaning of life out onto the road.

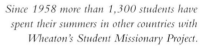

Since 1958 more than 1,300 students have spent their summers in other countries with Wheaton's Student Missionary Project.

In 1957 alumnus Ron Chase '56 returned to Wheaton as a speaker to challenge students to consider short-term summer missionary service. Ron's idea became the Student Missionary Project, and eventually a ministry of Wheaton's Office of Christian Outreach. Pictured here are children whom students taught in Alaska, 1959.

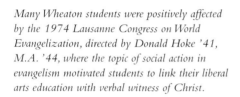

Few students find the Youth Hostel Ministry (YHM) experience easy. Many have described it as one of the most challenging summers of their life. But most are marked by memorable encounters.

Many Wheaton students were positively affected by the 1974 Lausanne Congress on World Evangelization, directed by Donald Hoke '41, M.A. '44, where the topic of social action in evangelism motivated students to link their liberal arts education with verbal witness of Christ.

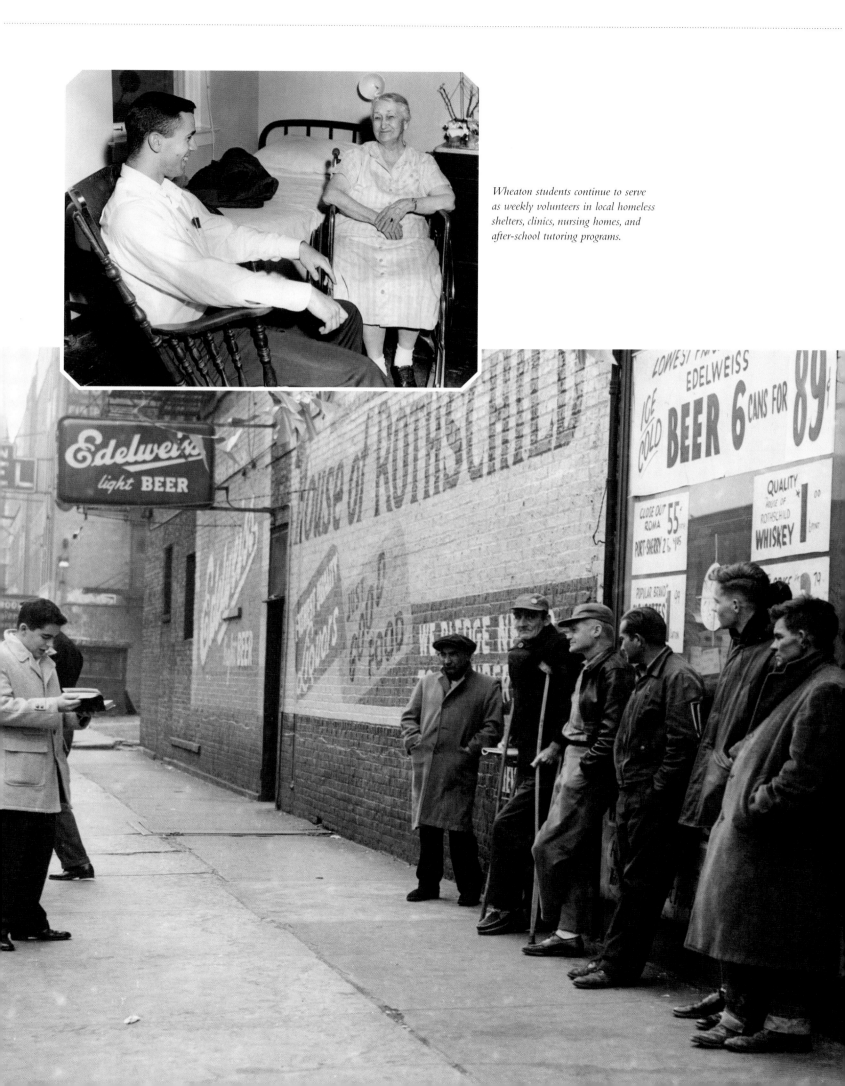

Wheaton students continue to serve as weekly volunteers in local homeless shelters, clinics, nursing homes, and after-school tutoring programs.

As Wheaton's early decades passed, residential life on campus flourished. Students who formerly boarded in local homes moved into newly constructed McManis and Evans halls. Men's Glee Club, Symphony Orchestra, Women's Chorale, and other musical groups performed on campus and on tours. Student publications, organizations, and clubs gave students opportunities to grow in abilities and leadership, and to refine and share what they believed.

Audiences in Europe, the British Isles, and across the U. S. have praised the Women's Chorale for its Christian witness and superlative sound.

In their early years, the Men's Glee Club and Women's Concert Chorale each made two trips a year, presenting concerts at schools and churches, urban and rural.

1930s campus fun

◄ *Wheaton emerged in the 1930s as the fastest growing college in America, becoming the largest liberal arts college in Illinois and the eighth largest in the U.S.*

In 2007 the Men's Glee Club, directed by Mary Hopper '73, celebrated its 100th year. The Glee Club has won multiple international choral competitions, and has performed for various heads of state, including President and Mrs. Reagan and Queen Juliana of the Netherlands.

The 1960s were years of social turbulence on Wheaton's campus, but also notable student achievement. In 1961 Wheaton students wrote 8 of the 20 first-place papers in the Atlantic magazine creative writing contest. In 1964, 51 percent of men and 84 percent of women entering the College were at or above the 90th percentile of their high school graduating class.

Student Government retreat at HoneyRock, 2009.

Archaeology Society students on site in Ashkelon, an ancient Israeli seaport occupied throughout history by Caananites, Philistines, Israelites, Babylonians, Greeks, Phoenicians, Romans, Persians, Arabian Muslims, and British.

Even while tackling critical issues on campus, members of Wheaton's 2008 Student Government take a moment to show their true colors.

WHEATON COLLEGE
FOR CHRIST AND HIS KINGDOM

The variety of student clubs invites friendships to flourish around widely diverse interests.

President Gerald R. Ford visited Wheaton in 1976, speaking for 12 minutes and then answering 8 questions. The next morning the Chicago Tribune said: "There was no sign of hostility as the students put the president under a 20-minute barrage of tough, incisive questions that shamed the professional reporters who question him daily." Today the campus climate at Wheaton continues to support healthy bipartisan conversations around faith and politics.

In on-campus residence halls, apartments, and houses, students learn in community with one another.

During the last century, the Tower and The Wheaton Record *have chronicled the issues and events of campus life. In more recent history* Kodon and The Pub *have emerged as student literary journals exploring the landscape of Christian faith and creative expression in contemporary society.*

Student organizations like Unidad Cristiana, the William Osborne Society, and Koinonia promote racial awareness, peer support, and leadership development among the students of Wheaton's campus.

In 1986 Adonya Seldon Little '90, Fred Dade '89, Jenai Davis Jenkins '89, and Vanessa Wilson '90 proposed the formation of the Gospel Choir. Since 1986 that choir has united Wheaton College students across ethnic and racial lines, ministering to churches, homeless shelters, schools, and prisons.

Since the beginning of the Iraq war (2003), 88 Reserve Officers Training Corps (ROTC) officers have graduated from Wheaton and gone on to serve in the U.S. armed forces.

Until 1966 with the performance of Macbeth, Wheaton College had never performed a "printed drama" on the theatrical stage. Now, Arena Theater is known as a setting where the "tragedy and triumph of human existence in this God-drenched world" shows itself not just on the stage, but in students who, while playing a character, recognize God's image in themselves.

"The eyes of the environmental world are on the church, but the eyes of the church are on my generation. We need to be a strong witness that will point others toward Christ."

—BEN LOWE '07, *member of the student creation care group A Rocha. In 2007, A Rocha hosted Wheaton's first Climate Change Summit attracting 80 attendees from 10 college campuses.*

Members of A Rocha, with Director of Environmental Studies Dr. Fred Van Dyke, lend a hand at Lincoln Marsh.

Members of student club Tikvaht Israel (Hope of Israel) stand outside a sukkot (tent) during the Feast of Booths.

In December 2002, Wheaton hosted U2 lead singer Bono and representatives from his organization Debt AIDS Trade Africa (DATA). Student response to this event sparked the organization of the first and one of the most active chapters of Student Global AIDS Campaign (SGAC) in the nation. SGAC has since sponsored several student AIDS summits with attendees from colleges around the country.

Following a long history of successful debate competition, Wheaton's Parliamentary Debate team was recently ranked 51st in the nation out of 955 teams in the National Parliamentary Tournament of Excellence.

Wheaton College athletics pushes students to win. "Winning is our goal each time we walk onto the court or step up to the plate," the athletics mission statement says. Underlying this aim is the greater goal of shaping lives for Jesus Christ.

Wheaton College, currently having won 167 conference championships, has not always promoted sports. When Charles Blanchard's daughter Mildred wrote to him in the late 1800s insisting that "young men needed exercise," Charles agreed, but felt they should get it in some practical way "such as sawing wood."

Yet by 1907, *The Record* reasoned: "There is a certain mutual and self confidence that may be gained in no way as when one bends every energy of mind and body to overcome obstacles and accomplish a certain objective whether directly or by assisting a team mate." The sport *The Record* was lobbying for was women's basketball.

One hundred years later, in the decade 2000-2010, Wheaton student-athletes earned 150 All-American selections and 24 Academic All-American honors. Over the years athletes also have engaged in service projects in the community and around the world—from hosting sports camps for local high school students, to building playgrounds at orphanages in South Africa, to playing street soccer with students in Botswana.

"It's not what you're doing that's important. It's who you're doing it with. . . . They'll realize it long after the fact." —Women's soccer coach, Pete Felske '86, commenting on his team's 2004 clinch of the NCAA Division III title.

Since 1965, Wheaton teams have taken nearly 50 sports ministry trips, often teaming up with alumni missionaries in the developing world.

"Wheaton is a unique institution. I think that it is the only institution in the world that really has as its basis an evangelical purpose of Christian education. Because of that, it calls for unique individuals to coach and serve here. You don't come to Wheaton to win national championships or to make a name for yourself. You come to Wheaton to serve student athletes who love Jesus."

—Men's soccer coach, Joe Bean, 2009

When Coach Bill Harris retired in 2009, he had the highest winning percentage of any men's basketball coach in Wheaton's history.

In his 1979 book Through Clouds and Sunshine, Coach Ed Coray '23 reflected on the early days of Wheaton men's basketball: "How would a modern basketball team react if they were shown a square basketball floor 40 feet by 40 feet with no out-of-bounds and heavily waxed? What would they think if . . . given turtleneck sweaters and pants down to the ankles for uniforms? Then told to go out on the floor to be refereed by the opponent's coach?" From this humble beginning, Wheaton rose to prominence in men's basketball. From 1994 to 2009 Wheaton players collected ten All-American honors and five Academic All-American accolades.

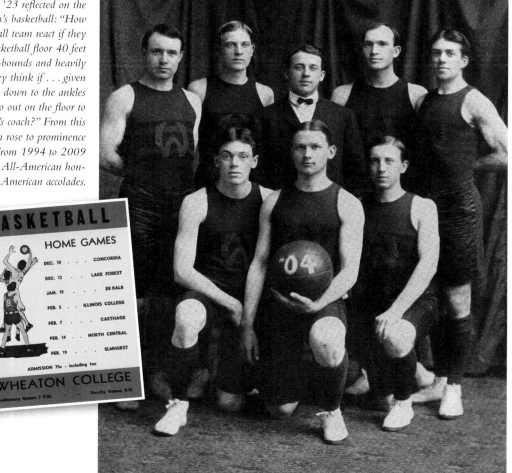

First Wheaton College baseball team—1915

Baseball was the first sport in which the men of Wheaton played teams from off campus. Alumni from the early years describe sand-filled burlap sacks for bases and a rock for home plate. In the 2008 and 2009 seasons, the baseball program set more than 20 school records, including school records for wins.

Controversy surrounded the game of football when it appeared on college campuses in the late 1800s because it was judged as rough, unrefined, and dangerous. The only comment The Record could offer on an unofficial game held in 1902 was, "Everyone reported fine treatment, a good time, and nobody killed." By the 1950s, Wheaton had developed a dominant football program, winning eight CCIW championships in the decade. Wheaton made its first-ever NCAA playoff appearance in 1995, and the program made five more post-season appearances from 2002-2008, under the guidance of alumnus Coach Mike Swider '77.

First Wheaton College football team—1915

◄ *In 1927 a sports editor for* The Record *referred to the football team as the "Crusaders," and the name stood for 73 years. But in 2000, Wheaton changed its athletic name to Thunder, and a new century of fan support came rolling in.*

Long before Title IX made equal funding for women's athletics mandatory, Wheaton students were lauding women's sports as patently good. "Don't you want to learn how to walk, how to stand, how to go up and down stairs, how, in a word, to gain complete control of your body?" wrote a student columnist in the December 1902 Record, urging all College women to become active participants on the women's basketball team.

Women athletes—1910

From 1986 to 2009, Wheaton won 62 CCIW championships in women's sports—almost twice as many championships as its nearest competitor. More recent additions to varsity sports include women's volleyball, softball, and water polo. The women's softball team produced its first All-American in 1997 and continues to build a competitive program.

Many consider Ruth Berg Leedy '32 the matriarch of women's athletics at Wheaton. She coached field hockey, the first women's sport to be played on an annual basis since the end of the women's basketball season in 1906, and provided leadership in an era before women's intercollegiate sports were standard. In 1989, Wheaton honored Coach Leedy for her 35 years of service by naming the new softball diamond after her.

When women's intercollegiate tennis was introduced in 1922, women players wore long white skirts and white middies with black scarves. At the end of the 1922 season, Margaret Mortenson '25, later Margaret Landon and author of Anna and the King of Siam, was one of the first two women in Wheaton history to receive a varsity letter. In 1938 and 1939, Beth Blackstone '40, who grew up in Nanjing, China, took the state championship in tennis two years in a row. In 1980, Wheaton freshman Jane Nelson '83 won the Association for Intercollegiate Athletics for Women (AIAW) Division III championship. In 1986 Nelson became Wheaton's women's tennis coach, guiding the team to 15 of the CCIW's first 24 conference championships in the sport, with four NCAA tournament appearances in her tenure, and mentoring 11 All-Americans as a coach.

Wheaton added women's soccer as a varsity sport in 1988, quickly becoming a strong program on the regional level and later the national level. The women's soccer program won its first Division III championship in 2004—Wheaton's first-ever national championship in a women's sport. Head coach Pete Felske '86 directed the program, winning back-to-back national titles in 2006 and 2007, as Wheaton became one of only three institutions ever to win three Division III championships.

"We do not argue that we desire the modern man to be a beef-eating Spartan or a Horatius, . . . but we do think it desirable that the modern man exercise more or less so that his bloodstream will be strong, so that his brain cells will be nourished, so that he can think. Therefore, let us have athletics. It is the only logical conclusion."

—Wheaton's first athletic director,
JASPER TURNBULL, 1914

Women's water polo

In 1984 and 1997, the Wheaton men's soccer team won the Division III championship. In 1996-98 Wheaton set a NCAA record for consecutive matches without a loss. Longtime Wheaton head coach Joe Bean retired in 2006 as the winningest coach in the history of collegiate men's soccer.

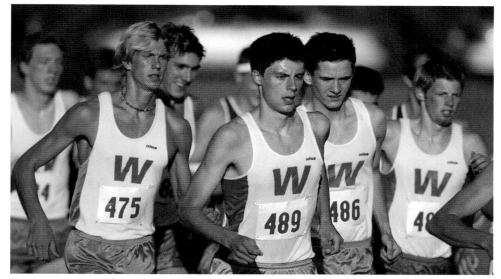

In the early days of men's cross country, the course was arranged so that the race would finish between halves of a football game. The competitors ran the length of the football field, with the finish line beneath the east goal posts. Wheaton hosted the NCAA men's cross country championships from 1958-74. Dan Henderson '80 won the NCAA Division III men's cross country championship in 1980. The Wheaton women's cross country program has won more CCIW championships than any other program in the league, winning a league-best ten titles from 1986-2008.

In 1972 swimmer Jon Lederhouse '74 won his second NCAA championship in the backstroke, returning to Wheaton soon after graduating to become coach of the men's and women's swimming programs. More than 70 Wheaton swimmers and divers have earned All-American honors during Lederhouse's tenure, with 7 Wheaton swimmers winning individual national championships.

Coach Bean applauds a great play at a men's soccer game.

The Sports and Recreation Complex built in 2000.

In 1954, Kikuo "Cookie" Moriya '55 won Wheaton's first NCAA individual championship in the two-mile run. Moriya came to Wheaton as a result of one of Gil Dodds' M.A. '48 trips through Japan with a Bible distribution society. Dodds led Moriya to the Lord and encouraged him to develop his spiritual education at Wheaton.

SEE GIL DODDS
World Champion Miler
Run Exhibition Race
In Dual Track Meet
UNIVERSITY of CHICAGO
vs.
WHEATON COLLEGE
MAY 14, 7:45 P.M.
GRANGE FIELD
Wheaton Community High School
•
Adults 65c   Students 30c   Children under 12, 10c
DON'T MISS IT!

Wheaton's track and field program has been in existence almost since the beginning of intercollegiate competition at the College. The men's and women's teams have acquired 11 national championships and produced more than 65 All-American honor students.

The women's golf team made its first NCAA championship appearance in 2009. In this same year, the men's golf team was recognized as an All-Academic team by the Golf Coaches Association of America.

During head coach Beth Baker's 24-year career, the women's basketball program has earned six CCIW championships and seven NCAA tournament appearances.

A coach and physical education instructor at Wheaton from 1961-2002, Marilyn Scribner brought the women's softball and volleyball programs into intercollegiate competition. The author of Free to Fight Back, *she has been a proponent and teacher of women's self-defense.*

The first full intercollegiate varsity wrestling schedule was implemented in 1929. In 1938 the wrestling program hosted the first Wheaton College Invitational. In 2000 the event was renamed the Pete Willson Wheaton Invitational, in honor of longtime wrestling coach Pete Willson '50. The historic tournament is the largest and oldest small-college wrestling tournament in America.

A buried cake, a hidden bench, uproarious cheers for each new class, and the thrill of the "Mastodon March." These are traditions that are maintained in the glimmer of late night hijinks and in class rivalry that is repeated year by year, but never the same way twice.

Going "Up the Tower." When it was first installed in Blanchard Hall's tower in 1872, the Blanchard bell summoned students to meals, chapel, class, and Sunday church. It pealed joyously for sports victories. In recent decades the ringing of the bell no longer announces class times, but rather engagements and marriages. Campus couples climb the tower stairs to ring the bell 21 times and scrawl their names among the crowded signatures of hundreds of others who have gone before them.

Senior Bench. According to dusty archives and oral tradition, the graduating class of 1912 is believed to have bequeathed the College a hefty concrete monument (the Bench) to solidify its place in the annals of their alma mater. The Bench was placed in front of Blanchard Hall, intended for use only by Wheaton seniors. Years passed uneventfully until 1949, when envious juniors from the class of 1950 devised a plot to make off with the top concrete slab of the Bench and hide it on campus. Thus began one of Wheaton's longest-standing and most passionate traditions. Every year juniors and seniors vie for control of the Bench, with the class in possession required to show it publicly three times a year. One of the more startling showings occurred when the class of 1959 displayed the Bench by suspending it from a helicopter over McCully field during halftime at a Homecoming football game.

Senior Cake. *The now abandoned Senior Cake tradition (1925-1943) required the senior class to bury a tinned fruitcake somewhere on campus on the first day of class. The junior class would have the school year to locate the cake. The search involved much enthusiasm for digging around campus. If the juniors did not "take the cake" the seniors would unearth it on Class Day (the last day of classes). A plaque on the far southwest corner of Blanchard Hall marks the spot where the cake from the class of 1938 was buried.*

Senior Sneak. *The name of this class-free day for seniors was always a bit of a misnomer since the sneak was usually expected and somewhat planned. In the early 1900s soon-to-graduate seniors escaped to a camp in the Michigan dunes. Today seniors are apt to attend a Cubs game at Wrigley Field or enjoy some other Chicago event or landmark.*

Freshman parade, 1940

The Stupe. *Think ice cream sodas, varsity sweaters, and high-backed wooden booths, and what you'll recall is the much-beloved "Stupe." The Stupe moved into the new Todd M. Beamer Student Center in 2002 and was soon joined by a second eatery, "Sam's," named in honor of retired Vice President of Student Development Sam Shellhamer. Here in this area of the Beamer Center students sip on fruit smoothies, shoot pool, talk politics, pick up their mail at CPO, or post a challenge on the Forum Wall.*

Dance. *It's not just square dancing anymore! In 2004, College Union in conjunction with the Student Activities Office began sponsoring several theme dances each year including ballroom, salsa, and swing.*

Spring Festival. *Throughout the 1940s and 1950s, the Spring Festival's pageant of costuming, stagecraft, and performance was one of the most anticipated events of the year. In more recent years, the festival has become a Class Films competition, an occasion that rolls out the red carpet for the student actors, screenwriters, and producers who create innovative films.*

"Brave Sons and Daughters True"

by Marilee A. Melvin '72, Executive Assistant to the President
(Vice President for Alumni Relations 1988-2005)

WHEATON'S 150-YEAR HISTORY MAY BEST BE UNDERSTOOD THROUGH THE LIVES OF ITS ALUMNI. NEARLY 50,000 MEN AND WOMEN HAVE EARNED A DEGREE FROM THE COLLEGE OR GRADUATE SCHOOL since Wheaton opened its doors, many of them making Wheaton's motto "For Christ and His Kingdom" their own. Like living manuscripts, their lives reveal the Light of the world. Jonathan Blanchard's vision for the abolition of human slavery in 1860 sprang from his allegiance to Jesus Christ. Many Wheaton alumni have demonstrated through the decades that, no longer enslaved to "self" but alive in Christ, they are free to serve others in His name. They view their lives as service with excellence and integrity, "seeking first the kingdom of God and His righteousness." Wheaton graduates validate Wheaton's mission.

Before coming to Wheaton I served on the staff of a U.S. President and his Attorney General. As I left Washington in 1988, Congressman Frank Wolf of Virginia asked me, "Why is it that my alma mater, graduating thousands of students each year, today has only one alumnus in the U.S. Congress, while 'little' Wheaton College has *three* alumni serving here (Paul Henry '63, Dennis Hastert '64, and Dan Coats '65, LL.D. '92), and yet a *fourth* is Chaplain of the U.S. Senate (Richard Halverson '39, LL.D. '58)?" Then he answered his own question, "It's because Wheaton

College, with an influence out of proportion to size, prepares leaders who know how to serve people. And now you get to go and serve them." Later that year Jim McDermott '57 successfully ran for Congress after serving with the State Department in Africa.

I made lifelong friends at Wheaton (1968-1972) in a time of intense cultural unrest. Unlike students of 2010, who carry whole libraries on their laptops and "text" their friends from across the dining hall, we typed term papers on portable typewriters, and phoned our friends with a rotary dial.

We pondered intractable problems, including the Vietnam War and the place of robotics. Our Wheaton professors saw these problems in historical perspective and from a biblical worldview, helping our minds awaken to meet life. Engaged in the difficult and joyous intellectual work of relating truth to life, they encouraged us to join in "the great conversation." I recall Dr. Richey Kamm explaining the superiority of a democratic and constitutional republic based on the rule of law: "We cannot live like flying saucers, but must have a system of government, and some

"The purpose of the Wheaton College Alumni Association shall be to unite all of the alumni of Wheaton College in a compact organization so that they may more effectively communicate with each other and with the College on matters of mutual interest, arrange for the alumni relations and in other ways foster and perpetuate the enthusiasm of the alumni for the College, and their interest in their fellow alumni."

As a Wheaton student, Marian Bulander '44 contributed a Record *newspaper column called "Belles on the Ball," featuring the accomplishments of Wheaton College women faculty and students. Shown here inscribing the Tower bell in her sophomore year, this picture was used in a 1942 Chicago Tribune feature story about the College, drawing "fan mail" to Marian from several dozen readers, mostly U.S. servicemen. Marian was secretary to the Alumni Association's first director, Ted Benson '38. In June 1946 she welcomed returning U.S. Naval officer Art Melvin '41 in the Association's fourth floor Blanchard office, and married him four months later during Homecoming weekend.*

systems are more just and humane than others." He gave me a framework to interpret my experience while serving at the White House and Department of Justice.

Wheaton's legacy includes an educational lineage dating back to its founder and his son, anchored in decades of fidelity to the College mission. I was taught the liberal arts by fellow alumni Art Holmes, Beatrice Batson, Ruth Leedy, Russell Mixter, and Gerry Hawthorne, who were taught in an earlier generation by alumni Edith Torrey, Elsie Storrs Dow, Darien Straw, Harvey and Dot Chrouser, and Merrill Tenney. Today's Wheaton students learn from those of my generation—Sharon Coolidge, Terry Perciante, Jill Lederhouse, and Mary Hopper, and also from *their* students Tim Larsen, Jenny Busch, and Stuart DeSoto. The character and scholarship of Wheaton professors impresses alumni for a lifetime, a joyful heritage deepening with each decade.

Wheaton alumni have been marked for life by Chapel messages, seed God

uses in cultivating hearts for His service. I recall Francis Schaeffer strolling across the Edman Chapel stage in his Swiss lederhosen, contending for "the reality of the infinite-personal God." From another generation I have my mother's handwritten notes taken in Pierce Chapel, dated January 21, 1944: "A Christian must choose to either live 'crucified with Christ,' or live with a split personality." God's Word expounded in Chapel helped shape my mother's Christ-like character, as it has generations of Wheaton students to this day.

The perspective of 150 years reveals the endurance of Wheaton relationships through succeeding generations. Nearly 20 percent of alumni find life mates at the College, and many others forge stabilizing and productive friendships that result in enterprises and ministries spanning generations.

The song lyrics of Wheaton's "Alma Mater" describe alumni as "brave sons and daughters true." For many, sharing the Good News of Jesus Christ as His ambassador is life's highest

calling. Billy Graham '43 may be the best known example. For more than six decades this graduate has proclaimed God's reconciliation with mankind to millions across the globe. Seven decades ago when Billy and his classmate Ruth Bell '43 were students at Wheaton and planning to marry, could they have dreamed God would use Billy to proclaim the Word of Life on every continent, and talk with kings, queens, presidents, popes, and prime ministers? Similar stories abound of Wheatonites being used of God through 150 years to "preach the gospel" while serving in a full range of vocations and professions. Alumnus David Howard '49, M.A. '52 has captured part of this story in his book *From Wheaton to the Nations* (2001).

An explosion of interest to share the gospel, fueled through student revivals in the 20th century, encouraged hundreds of alumni to serve in missions. Other alumni determined to help fund the Great Commission. Ken '41, LL.D. '66 and Jean Hermann Hansen '41 had

"Grandpa Charlie" (President Charles Blanchard 1870) spends an afternoon with three of his grandchildren, the children of Harold 1909 and Rachel Blanchard MacKenzie 1902. He sits with Jean MacKenzie Airhart '35, Margaret Delphia MacKenzie Moffett '38, and Harold MacKenzie '36. Photo circa 1916.

hoped to serve in China. When they found they could not go themselves, they set about enabling their Wheaton friends to go. As the idea of missions changed, Christian leaders from developing nations came to Wheaton for advanced training, and returned to their homes to share the gospel. Many of these stories are captured in *Stones of Remembrance I* and *II*, published by the College in 1995 and 2006.

From Wheaton's earliest days alumni have stayed connected to one another and the College. Yearbooks from the 1890s describe annual meetings at Commencement. During Wheaton's first 50 years, alumni formed organizations with a written constitution and the selection of officers to "further the interests of the College and its former students." From 1921, alumni volunteers organized fellowship groups in Rockford, Chicago, and New York. Throughout the College's 150 years, alumni have helped arrange events on campus and around the globe. Today they meet for reunions on campus,

connect online, travel through a worldwide travel program, and enjoy an annual retreat for "seniors" at Honey-Rock. The enthusiasm and support of alumni volunteers is a secret strength of Wheaton's Alumni Association.

In 1944 the Alumni Association was incorporated, with the blessing of the College, to give voice to the growing organization of graduates. Top among their aims was encouraging alumni financial gifts to assist the faculty. Generous alumni giving in those early years prompted later College administrations to make faculty support an ongoing priority. More than 75 percent of alumni have contributed financially.

Alumni loyalty for their alma mater is not unusual, but fifteen decades of rigorous, Christ-centered, liberal arts education at Wheaton have resulted in a unique legacy. Nearly one-fifth of the freshman class today comes from alumni families, including students descended seven generations from Jonathan Blanchard. The workforce at Wheaton is nearly 36 percent alumni,

and more than three quarters of the trustee board are graduates.

Every year, early on commencement day, Wheaton's newest graduates and their families meet in Edman Chapel for a last worship service with their professors. The President challenges these fledgling alumni to live for Jesus Christ and His kingdom purposes. At last the seniors sing *a capella* the final three verses of "May the Mind of Christ My Savior." May this prayer be true for them, and remain Wheaton's legacy until Jesus returns.

May the love of Jesus fill me
As the waters fill the sea;
Him exalting, self abasing,
This is victory.
May I run the race before me,
Strong and brave to face the foe,
Looking only unto Jesus
As I onward go.
May His beauty rest upon me,
As I seek the lost to win,
And may they forget the channel,
Seeing only Him.

Alumni of the Year for Distinguished Service to Alma Mater

1953   **DR. ENOCK C. DYRNESS '23**
Registrar; Vice President of Faculty
MIGNON BOLLMAN MACKENZIE '33
Professor, Music

1954   **HERMAN A. FISCHER, JR. 1903**
Attorney; Trustee

1955   **DR. EDWARD R. SCHELL '22, LL.D. '49,**
M.A. '53, *Dean, Wheaton College Academy*

1956   **DR. STANLEY W. OLSON '34, LL.D. '53**
Medical School Dean; Trustee

1957   **CORINNE R. SMITH '34, B.M.E. '37**
Dean of Women

1958   **DR. RUSSELL L. MIXTER '28**
Chairman, Biology Department

1959   **EDWARD A. CORAY '23**
Executive Director, Alumni Association

1960   **DR. PAUL M. WRIGHT '26**
Chairman, Chemistry Department

1961   **DR. P. KENNETH GIESER '30, LL.D. '76**
Ophthalmologist; Trustee

1962   **DR. ARTHUR H. VOLLE '38**
Professor, Education

1963   **CHARLES B. WEAVER '24,** *Banker; Trustee*

1964   **DR. CLARENCE B. HALE '28**
Chairman, Foreign Language Department

1965   **DR. CLARENCE B. WYNGARDEN '32**
Wheaton College Physician

1966   **DR. ANGELINE JANE BRANDT '27**
Professor of Mathematics; Counselor

1967   **DR. DONALD C. BOARDMAN '38**
Chairman, Geology Department

1968   **HARVEY C. CHROUSER '34**
Director, Physical Education, Athletics

1969   **RUTH BERG LEEDY '32**
Professor, Physical Education

1970   **DR. BERNARD A. NELSON '31**
Chairman, Chemistry Department

1971   **DR. EVAN D. WELSH '27, D.D. '55,** *Chaplain*

1972   **EDWARD A. CORDING '33**
Director, Public Relations, Conservatory

1973   **MARTHA COLE BAPTISTA '45**
Assistant Dean of Students
DR. ROBERT C. BAPTISTA, SR. '44
Vice President, Academic Affairs

1974   **DR. CYRIL E. LUCKMAN '37**
Professor, Biology

1975   **DAVID L. ROBERTS '41**
Director of Development

1976   **DR. HUDSON T. ARMERDING '41,** *President*

1977   **CARTER H. CODY '40**
Assistant in Development
LEROY H. PFUND '49
Coach; Director, Alumni Relations

1978   **DR. ARTHUR F. HOLMES '50, M.A. '52**
Professor, Philosophy

1979   **DR. HAROLD A. FIESS '39**
Professor, Chemistry

1980   **HOWARD W. WHITE '41,** *Controller*

In 2006 Dick '59 and Marge Nystrom Gieser '59 made another annual visit to the Sudan where Dick helped local medical doctors with eye operations, and Marge worked with local people to create educational murals on the walls of buildings. Dick and Marge say they receive more than they give on these annual global journeys.

Physicist, professor, missionary, and administrator, Jim Kraakevik '48, seen here with his wife Lynn, served Wheaton in various academic and administrative roles spanning 40 years. He later served as the director of the Billy Graham Center for 12 years.

In 2001 Ruth Bamford '50, once Wheaton's dean of student programs, joined a group of senior alumni volunteers in initiating "Northwoods Adventure," an annual week-long retreat at HoneyRock. Today nearly 100 alumni age 55 and older meet each fall in Wisconsin's beautiful Northwoods for new learning opportunities and rich fellowship.

The word alumni *derives from the Latin* alere, *meaning "to nourish or nurture." Wheaton and its alumni are involved in a lifelong relationship of mutual care, interest, help, and friendship. Alumni receive the blessing of relationships with professors, mentors and coaches, classmates, and friends. Blessed by rich relationships, they in turn help "nourish" the College. And they have ably done so throughout Wheaton's history with their fiscal and material support, prayer, wise counsel (including constructive criticism!), enthusiasm, and loyalty.*

Roger Sandberg, Jr. '00 spent three years as the south Sudan country director for Samaritan's Purse before joining MedAir in 2005 to continue in relief work responding to famines, floods, and medical outbreaks in Central Africa. He and his wife, Rebecca Seneff Sandberg '99, worked out of Nairobi, Kenya, when their children were small, where Rebecca helped with Amani ya Juu, a sewing-marketing-training project for marginalized women in Africa.

Dr. David Zac Niringiye M.A. '87, assistant bishop of the Anglican church in Kampala, Uganda, spoke at Commencement, 2006. His addresses challenged graduates to serve those on the fringes of society. He cautioned them "to avoid becoming spectators of the future" and to "engage with the margins."

As the developmental relief coordinator for Food for the Hungry, Sara Sywulka '95 has traveled the world to help people in greatest need—including the thousands of people displaced by the 2005 earthquake in Pakistan that killed more than 73,000 people.

Alumni of the Year for Distinguished Service to Alma Mater

1981   HELEN SIML deVETTE '45, M.A. '49
        Professor, English
        DR. ROBERT O. deVETTE '41, M.A. '49
        Professor, Spanish; Director, Admissions
1982   REV. H. LeROY PATTERSON '40, *Chaplain*
1983   HENRI E. ECKHARDT '40
        Planned Giving Officer
        ROBERT D. NOLES '40
        Planned Giving Officer
1984   REGINALD GERIG '42
        Professor, Conservatory of Music
        DR. JACK SWARTZ '52
        Professor, Physical Education
1985   DR. GERALD F. HAWTHORNE '51, M.A. '54
        Professor, Greek
        ELEANOR P. PAULSON '47
        Professor, Speech
1986   DONALD L. CHURCH '57
        Professor, Physical Education
        RICHARD E. GERIG '49
        Director, Public Affairs
1987   DR. MELVIN E. LORENTZEN '49
        Professor, Communications
        PETER R. WILLSON '50
        Professor, Physical Education
1988   GLADYS C. CHRISTENSEN '49
        Professor, Conservatory of Music
        KENNETH T. WESSNER '44, LL.D. '90
        Business Executive; Trustee
1989   RUTH E. BAMFORD '50
        Associate Dean, Student Development
        JEAN RUMBAUGH '49
        Staff, Registrar's Office
1990   DR. RAYMOND H. BRAND '50
        Professor, Biology
        DAVID C. HELSER '58
        Staff, Constituent Records
1991   NANCY ELLEN DERCK LONG '72
        Staff, HoneyRock
        WILLIAM C. LONG, JR. '72
        Director, HoneyRock
1992   DR. EDWIN A. HOLLATZ G.S. '55
        Professor, Communications
        DR. JAMES H. KRAAKEVIK '48
        Director, Billy Graham Center
        ROBERT D. SHUSTER '73
        Director, Billy Graham Center Archives
1993   IVY T. OLSON '39, *Librarian*
        GUNTHER H. "BUD" KNOEDLER '51
        Businessman; Trustee
1994   DR. DELBURT H. NELSON '36
        Physician; Trustee
        DR. JOHN A. GRATION M.A. '52
        Professor, Missions
1995   DR. TERENCE H. PERCIANTE '67
        Professor, Math/Computer Science
1996   RUTH JAMES CORDING '33
        College Archivist

"Sixty-six years ago Jonathan Blanchard founded Wheaton College, 'For Christ and His Kingdom,' pointing out its position, as he said, midway between the two oceans, and midway between Europe and the Orient. Time has justified his dream of influence, for from every continent come our students, and to every land they go with the message and the power of the Christian life. . . . Through the past generation Wheaton has remained an accredited college, and at the same time kept true to distinctly Christian standards of faith and practice."

—PRESIDENT JAMES OLIVER BUSWELL, JR.
Inaugural address, *June 15, 1926*

A packed audience at an alumni symposium during Alumni Weekend 2008 heard Drs. Mark Noll '68, Nathan Hatch '68, and John Piper '68 in a panel discussion titled "1968, A Year in Crisis: Evangelical Churches Then and Now."

Concerned that his ten children would not understand the King James Bible with great depth at their young ages, Dr. Kenneth Taylor '38, LITT. D. '65 began paraphrasing the New Testament epistles into conversational English for his children as he rode the train to and from Chicago. In 1962 he founded Tyndale House Publishers as a means of publishing The Living Bible.

Rodney '84 and Hasana Pennant Sisco '86, with sons Juwan and Jabari, gather with other alumni for a reunion photo. Rodney directs the College's office of multicultural development, and Hasana is director of global safety, health, environment, and compliance at Nalco, the world's leading water treatment and process improvement company.

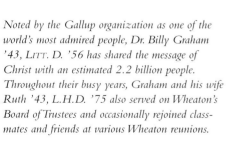

Noted by the Gallup organization as one of the world's most admired people, Dr. Billy Graham '43, LITT. D. '56 has shared the message of Christ with an estimated 2.2 billion people. Throughout their busy years, Graham and his wife Ruth '43, L.H.D. '75 also served on Wheaton's Board of Trustees and occasionally rejoined classmates and friends at various Wheaton reunions.

Alumni of the Year for Distinguished Service to Alma Mater

1996　REV. DENNIS K. MASSARO '75, M.A. '84
Director, Office of Christian Outreach

1997　C. WILLIAM "BILL" POLLARD '60
Business Executive; Trustee
JUDY WYNGARDEN POLLARD '60
College Hostess

1998　GEORGIA I. DOUGLASS '70, M.A. '94
Director, Marketing Communications

1999　DR. IVAN J. FAHS '54, Professor, Sociology
JOYCE EVANS FAHS '54
Staff, Registrar's Office

2000　DR. GEORGE "BUD" WILLIAMS M.A. '66
Coach; Staff, HoneyRock

2001　DR. HERB WOLF '60
Professor, Graduate Theological Studies

2002　DR. MARK A. NOLL '68, Professor, History

2003　DR. WALTER A. ELWELL '59, M.A. '61
Professor, Graduate Theological Studies

2004　JAMES M. LANE '52
Business Executive; Trustee
ARLYNE NELSON LANE '52, College Hostess
BETTY BURTNESS KNOEDLER '50
College Hostess

2005　DR. WALTER C. KAISER, JR. '55, B.D. '58
Seminary President; Trustee
DR. ROBERT L. BRABENEC '60
Professor, Math/Computer Science

2006　DR. ROGER W. LUNDIN '71
Professor, English
MARILEE A. MELVIN '72
Vice President, Alumni Relations

2007　DR. E. BEATRICE BATSON, M.A. '47
Professor, English

2008　DR. DEAN E. ARNOLD '64
Professor, Sociology/Anthropology

2009　DR. DAVID E. JOHNSTON '65
Senior Vice President

2010　DR. MARY HOPPER '73
Professor, Conservatory of Music

Alumni of the Year for Distinguished Service to Society

1953　DR. JOHN R. BROBECK '36, LL.D. '60
Physician; Professor

1954　HOWELL G. EVANS '22
Business Executive

1955　DR. J. LAURENCE KULP '42, Scientist

1956　DR. STEPHEN W. PAINE '30, LL.D. '39
College President

1957　DR. BILLY GRAHAM '43, LITT.D. '56
Evangelist

1958　DR. RUTH KRAFT STROHSCHIEN '27
Pediatrician

1959　DR. PAUL E. ADOLPH '23
Physician; Missionary; Author

Dr. Warren Cooper's '88 work with World Medical Mission affords him opportunity to administer relief and minister the gospel through medicine. He is pictured here in Lui, Sudan, with a young patient. Warren once said about his work, "The ultimate goal is to live out your life in such a way that your faith and your 'daily work' are manifestations of the same thing."

Alumni stories have been recorded for more than 80 years in the "Alumni News." For fellow alumni these stories have been a source of great encouragement and validation of the College mission. Alexander MacLeod '23 edited the first magazine in 1929. For a quarter of the magazine's history, Georgia Douglass '70, M.A. '94 has edited and created Wheaton magazine, an award-winning publication that is read by Wheatonites in more than 120 nations and on four continents.

Margaret Mortenson Landon '25 and her husband, Kenneth Landon '24, were missionaries in Thailand from 1927 to 1937. In 1944 she published the book that became the basis for the musical The King and I. Kenneth served the U.S. Department of State as an advisor on Southeast Asia for many years.

David Roberts '41 assisted his classmate, Wheaton's fifth president Hudson Armerding, for many years as "Special Assistant to the President." He also helped build Wheaton's development office for 37 years.

"It's hard to imagine a better vocation for reaching the lost than the chaplaincy," said Cpt. David Curlin '90 about leaving the church pulpit for the foxholes of the U.S. Army as a military chaplain.

Alumni of the Year for Distinguished Service to Society

1960   DR. EVERETT D. SUGARBAKER '31
Physician; Author

1961   DR. CARL F. H. HENRY '38, M.A. '41, LITT.D. '68
Theologian; Journalist

1962   DR. HOWARD F. MOFFETT '39, LL.D. '68
Medical Missionary; Evangelist
MARGARET MACKENZIE MOFFETT '38
Medical Missionary; Evangelist

1963   ELISABETH HOWARD ELLIOT GREN '48
Missionary; Author

1964   DR. LAWRENCE H. ANDRESON '35
Leader in Church, Youth, and Medical Work

1965   DR. SAMUEL H. MOFFETT '38
Leader in Christian Missions
DR. ELIZABETH JADERQUIST PADDON '26
Leader in Christian Missions

1966   DR. TITUS M. JOHNSON '28
Medical Missionary

1967   DR. DAVID H. PAYNTER '44
Education Administrator

1968   LYNDON R. HESS '31, *Missionary*
RUTH DeVELDE HESS '31, *Missionary*

1969   NORRIS A. ALDEEN '38
Corporation President

1970   HAROLD G. MORDH '48
Superintendent, Union Gospel

1971   DR. PAUL B. STAM '44
Industrial Research Executive

1972   DR. DONALD E. McDOWELL '46
Surgeon; Missionary
DR. ELOIS R. FIELD '45
Nurse; Teacher; Administrator

1973   DR. ELEANOR SOLTAU '38
Missionary; Physician; Administrator
DR. PAUL W. GAST '52, *Scientist*

1974   DOROTHY HORTON GALDE '34
College Professor
DR. JOHN ELSEN '42, *Physician*
VIRGINIA CULVER ELSEN '42, *Counselor*

1975   REV. CHARLES HESS '25
Missionary; Bible Translator

1976   RUTH HEGE '30
Missionary; Author; Speaker
DR. O. GRANT WHIPPLE '34
Christian Camping, Youth Work

1977   REV. DAVID M. HOWARD '49, M.A. '52
Missionary; Missions Director
DR. KENNETH N. TAYLOR '38, LITT.D. '65
Author; Publisher

1978   DR. VIOLET E. BERGQUIST-REDDING '39
College Professor
REV. GROVER C. WILLCOX '44, M.DIV. '46
Pastor

1979   DR. WILLARD M. ALDRICH '31
Bible College Founder and President

1980   GERTRUDE E. KELLOGG GAMMON '44
Missionary; Translator

A former Alumni Association president and the only 1954 graduate to attend all ten of his class reunions, Ray Smith '54 proudly declares, "I'm a Wheaton guy and everyone knows it." Passionate about Wheaton athletics, Ray never scored a touchdown at McCully stadium, but "the Scribe" captured Wheaton victories with his pen. He never hit a home run on Lawson field, but he's connected alumni to their Wheaton "home" for more than a half century.

Ken Hansen '41, LL.D. '66 was recruited a year after graduation to join Chicago businessman Marion Wade in the development of a carpet cleaning company, CleanMaster. Within a decade Ken had recruited dozens of Wheaton friends and alumni to help build ServiceMaster as a successful franchising corporation. Ken Wessner '44, LL.D. '90 and Bill Pollard '60, along with many other alumni, continued to develop the company in succeeding decades.

O. Maxine Bates '70, pounds grain with a Nigerian friend, Ruda, in 1945. Maxine served with SIM in Nigeria and used her missionary furloughs over twenty years to complete coursework enabling her to earn a degree from Wheaton. Near the end of her studies at the College she attended classes with a Nigerian national she had led to Christ.

For Alumni Weekend 2009, Charlotte Truesdell Marcy '35 and her daughter, Pearl Marcy '59, flew in from Honduras, where they serve as missionaries.

While Ed Coray '23 was president of the Student Council during his senior year, students came up with the idea of hosting an annual "Homecoming"—a tradition that has continued from 1923 to the present. Ed Coray himself missed only two homecomings between his graduation and his death shortly before his class's 70th reunion.

John Elmer Phillips '28 returned to Wheaton for his 65th class reunion and recaptured a moment from decades earlier.

Alumni of the Year for Distinguished Service to Society

A home in Tegucigalpa, Honduras, vibrates with life, love, and active boys serving soup kitchens, camps, and other projects. The Micah Project, a group home started by Michael Miller '94, is a safe community for boys who have left a life of hunger and drugs on the streets in order to learn and grow in a "family."

After the Commencement ceremony, three Wheaton graduates—and new alumni—celebrate. (l to r) Julie Diller Sawyer '90, John Douglass '90, and Kristin Widman Gustafson '90.

Dr. Taylor McKenzie's '54 teacher, Willard Bass '34, recruited him to come to Wheaton from the Navajo reservation where he was raised. As a member of Wheaton's track team Taylor broke speed records. He was the first member of his tribe to graduate from medical school and the first Navajo Nation surgeon general. He later served as vice president of the Navajo Nation.

Dr. Melvin Banks, Sr. '58, M.A. '60, LITT.D. '93 (left) founded Urban Ministries, Inc., the largest independent, African American-owned and operated Christian media company. He served as a College trustee for 17 years. Wayne Gordon '75 (right), motivated by God's love and justice, had a vision for racial reconciliation and serving the urban poor. With John Perkins LL.D. '80 he founded the Christian Community Development Association using biblical and practical principles to address poverty.

Dr. Arthur Amman '58 has poured three decades of energy into researching HIV/AIDS in an effort to slow the pandemic in some of the world's poorest countries. In 1981 he discovered and confirmed the first case of AIDS contracted through a blood transfusion—a realization that forced the world's blood bank industry to examine their stores with much greater care.

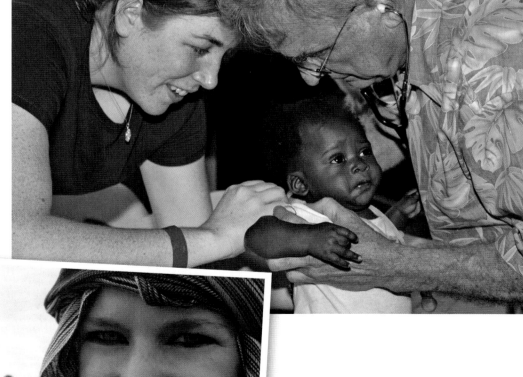

Michael Hudson '89 captures Wheaton athletic history through his telephoto lens.

Megan Pavlischek '09 received a Fulbright full grant to conduct research in Morocco for one year after graduation.

Alumni of the Year for Distinguished Service to Society

1992 DR. J. FRANK CASSEL '38, *Scholar; Scientist*
CHARLES D. HOLSINGER '49, M.A. '53
Missionary
BETTY HERMANSEN HOLSINGER '49
Missionary

1993 DR. KENNETH N. HANSEN '41, LL.D. '66
Businessman
DR. RICHARD B. STROM '44, M.A. '48
Missionary; Teacher
DONNA YOUNG STROM '46
Missionary; Teacher

1994 VIRGINIA A. DETER '46, *Missionary*
REV. DR. BRYANT KIRKLAND '35, *Pastor*

1995 DR. GEORGE KELSEY '52, M.A. '55
Linguist; Missionary
MARTHA NYSTEDT KELSEY '55
Linguist; Missionary
DR. ROBERT P. EVANS '39
Missionary; Mission Founder
JEANETTE GRUNER EVANS '40
Missionary; Mission Founder

1996 DR. HOWARD HENDRICKS '46
Educator; Theologian
JEANNE WOLFE HENDRICKS '48
Theologian; Author
DR. BURWELL "PAT" M. KENNEDY '48
Missionary; Physician

1997 DR. TED W. WARD '51, *Educator*
MARGARET HOCKETT WARD '52
Educator

1998 DR. JOHN W. NELSON '63, D.MUS. '89
Music Director, Conductor
ANITA JOHNSEN NELSON '64
Musician; Manager
CHARLES HOGREN '58, *Lawyer; Advocate*

1999 JANE MCNALLY '39, M.A. '44
Missionary; Author
THE HONORABLE DANIEL R. COATS '65
U.S. Congressman, Senator
MARSHA CRAWFORD COATS '66, *Counselor*

2000 DR. TAYLOR MCKENZIE '54
*Vice President and Medical Officer,
Navajo Nation*

2001 ADA LUM '50, M.A. '52, *Missionary; Teacher*
REV. BURTON SMITH '51, *Missionary*
AUDREY ERICKSON SMITH '51, *Missionary*

2002 THE HONORABLE J. DENNIS HASTERT '64
U.S. Congressman, Speaker of the House
DR. LOUIS L. CARTER, JR. '61
Medical Missionary; Teacher
LISA BROSIOUS BEAMER '91
Businesswoman
TODD M. BEAMER '91 (POSTHUMOUSLY)
Businessman

2003 LUCI DECK SHAW '53
Poet; Essayist; Teacher; Publisher
DR. RICHARD N. LONGENECKER '53, M.A. '56
Theologian; Teacher; Author

Ed Coray '23 retired from coaching at Wheaton in 1950 to serve for 20 more years as the Alumni Association's second alumni director. In 1953 he and the Alumni Board established the annual Distinguished Service Awards. During his tenure he initiated the Alumni Club program; helped raise funds from alumni to build Alumni Gymnasium (now the Edward A. Coray Memorial Gymnasium), Memorial Student Center, and Edman Chapel; and carried on a vast correspondence with alumni.

Barry Pea '80 was executive vice president and general counsel of Immunex Corporation, negotiating the biggest merger in biotechnology history with Amgen in 2002. He was pivotal in creating the contractual and commercial infrastructure for Enbrel, the world's top-selling biotech product. He is a Wheaton parent, chairman of the Board of Visitors, and is still active as a biotech legal consultant.

Chaplain Evan Welsh '27, once a member of Wheaton's "Crusader" football team in the 1920s, was frequently seen during his long tenure as Alumni Chaplain on the sidelines at football competitions, cheering on student athletes, as in this photo with Chaplain Pat Patterson '40.

"Wheaton College is a thumbprint institution that marks its graduates for life. When I ask what most influenced them, alumni never mention the president, or the administration, or the buildings, but rather their friends, their professors and coaches, and Chapel."

—PRESIDENT DUANE LITFIN

In 1958 Don Church '57 began his service at Wheaton as the track and cross country coach, and retired 39 years later as associate professor of kinesiology. "One of the most important lessons I learned at Wheaton," he says, "was how significant good role models are in one's life. I have learned from many people here at Wheaton, as well as seen how important faculty and staff are in the lives of students." Always an encourager, Don began, and for many years administered, a program for faculty missionary service overseas.

Incorporated by the State of Illinois in 1944, the first Wheaton College Alumni Association board was led by Ken Gieser '30, LL.D. '76, and alumni director, Ted Benson '38. As of Wheaton's Sesquicentennial, sixty men and women have served as Association presidents, and six as alumni directors. Following Ted Benson was Ed Coray '23 (1950-1970); and then John Taylor '45, M.A. '47 (1970-1975), LeRoy "Lee" Pfund '49 (1975-1987), Marilee Melvin '72 (1988-2005), and Cindra Stackhouse Taetzsch '82 (2006-present). Four Alumni Association directors are pictured in the 1988 Homecoming parade: John Taylor, Lee Pfund, Ed Coray, and Marilee Melvin. Cindra Stackhouse Taetzsch is shown in the inset.

Alumni of the Year for Distinguished Service to Society

2004	DR. HAROLD P. ADOLPH '54
	Physician; Missionary; Author
	BONNIE JO ADELSMAN ADOLPH '55
	Missionary; Teacher; Administrator
2005	DR. JOHN C. "JACK" SWANSON '49
	Administrator; Counselor; Missionary
2006	ELISABETH "LIZ" ISAIS '46
	Journalist; Editor; Teacher; Missionary
2007	DR. ARTHUR J. AMMANN '58
	Physician; Missionary
2008	DR. AKIKO OSHIRO MINATO, M.A. '60
	Scholar; Writer; Speaker; Dean
2009	DR. GREG LIVINGSTONE '62, M.A. '68
	Missionary
	SALLY COLTMAN LIVINGSTONE '62
	Missionary
2010	DR. WAYNE "COACH" GORDON '75
	Pastor; Teacher; Coach

Alumni of the Year for Distinguished Service to Family

1994	GENEVA VAN DYKE SUGARBAKER '33
1996	DOROTHY RANDALL NORBECK '50
	DR. DAVID NORBECK, SR. '47
1997	RAYMOND E. BADGERO, M.A. '81
	LOIS OSTERHUS BADGERO, M.A. '81
1998	DAVID WILLIAMS '68
	SHARON BULLOCK WILLIAMS '68
1999	RUTH BELL GRAHAM '43, L.H.D. '75
2000	DR. KENNETH TAYLOR '38, LITT.D. '65
	MARGARET WEST TAYLOR '39
2003	DR. WALTER B. HULL '59
	NANCY RUTHERFORD HULL '60

Lifetime Friendship Award

2000	OLENA MAE HENDRICKSON WELSH '41
2004	RAY H. SMITH '54

With five tackles, one assist, two interceptions, and a quarterback sack against defending Super Bowl champions, the Pittsburgh Steelers, Andy Studebaker '08 became the first Wheaton athlete to start in an NFL football game. Andy plays linebacker for the Kansas City Chiefs.

President of Tokyo Christian Women's University, visiting fellow at Harvard University, and board member of World Vision Japan, Dr. Akiko Oshiro Minato M.A. '60 urged the Wheaton class of 2008 in her commencement address to go out into the world as peacemakers—strong words from one who was raised in militant pre-WWII Japan, and then lived through a U.S. airstrike on her school. Wheaton's President Edman married Akiko and her late husband, Hiroshi, at St. John's Lutheran Church in Wheaton.

Rev. Jasper Bacon (right) '82, executive director of In His Steps Ministries, a nonprofit organization to support at-risk children, juvenile offenders, and their families, and Rev. Randy Gruendyke (center) '82, college pastor at Taylor University, collaborate during a Homecoming weekend.

Nate Saint '50

Seeking to fulfill Christ's Great Commission to "go and make disciples of all nations," missionaries Jim Elliot '49, Ed McCully '49, Nate Saint '50, Roger Youderian, and Peter Fleming were killed by Waodani tribesmen in Ecuador in 1956. From left to right: Ed and Marilou McCully (with their son), Pete Fleming, Emma Guikema, and Elisabeth and Jim Elliot.

Nate Saint '50 dreamed of serving in mission aviation as a Wheaton student. Many years later his son Steve '72 returned with his family to continue sharing God's love with the Waodani people. The story of the Saints, and the 1956 event that gripped the attention of the world, is portrayed in the 2006 feature film, "The End of the Spear."

From her early experience as a teacher, Bonnie Pruett Wurzbacher '77 had a natural gift for identifying individuals' skills and placing them in roles where those strengths were best suited. As senior vice president of global customer leadership at Coca-Cola Company, she not only builds strong teams, but also looks to strengthen communities.

Do "Wheaties" float in the Dead Sea? Apparently, they do! While studying Arabic and working in Amman, Jordan, Julia Wallin '09 welcomed friends and fellow Wheaton students Alex Leo '11 and Anna Westlund '11 as they came through Jordan with their Middle East study abroad program. Their reading material as they swam in the Dead Sea was Wheaton magazine.

Kingdom, Come!

by Dr. Philip G. Ryken '88, Eighth President of Wheaton College

WHEATON COLLEGE HAS MORE THAN A HISTORY. IT ALSO HAS AN ESCHATOLOGY— a set of biblical convictions about God's plans for the end of the world and the everlasting kingdom of Jesus Christ.

It has been this way from the outset. When Jonathan Blanchard first came to help carve a Christian college out of the Illinois prairie, he was explicit about his intentions. Why did he come to Wheaton? "The chief reason," said President Blanchard, speaking in 1891 at his 80th birthday party, "was I believed the Lord had need of Wheaton College, to aid in preparing the way for His coming."

From the beginning, then, the College has been getting ready for the very end, when Christ will come again. "In my beginning is my end," T. S. Eliot wrote in "East Coker," the second poem of his *Four Quartets*. Eliot meant, in part, that the culmination of his existence was bound up in his inception. So it has been for Wheaton College. When we were founded as a kingdom institution, we were given purposes that extend all the way to the end of the world, and then on into eternity.

As we wait for our King to come again, we find ourselves busy working for a kingdom that will never end. Drawn by the revelation of a glorious future, we are preparing the way for the Second Coming of Jesus Christ. Loving the liberal arts, pursuing the life of the Christian mind, integrating our learning with our faith, answering God's call to nearly every form of vocation and ministry—serving God in the home, the church, and the world—this is all kingdom work. In other words, it is all work (and play!) that demonstrates the present Lordship of the risen Christ over His creation, and at the same time shows the possibility of redemption for a fallen world.

Our calling, "For Christ and His Kingdom," enables us to anticipate at least some of the things that will happen in days to come. We can never know the whole future, of course, but we can and do know a good deal about the future of the kingdom of God.

To the extent that Wheaton College remains a "kingdom institution," therefore, the Bible tells us what the future may bring.

To begin, we know that the kingdom will spread. According to the promise of Jesus, the gospel of His kingdom "will be preached in the whole world as a testimony to all nations, and then the end will come" (Matt. 24:14, NIV). Wheaton College is part of this global work, not only by helping to prepare alumni for service on a number of mission fields, but also by serving as salt and light in all places where God calls members of the Wheaton family to go.

The spread of the kingdom draws us closer into fellowship with the worldwide people of God, as our connection to Christ simultaneously establishes a connection with His people in every place. In the words of Wheaton alumnus John Piper '68, "All of history is moving toward one great

goal: the white-hot worship of God and His Son among all the peoples of the earth."

As a Christ-centered, kingdom-minded college, Wheaton has always been moving toward that goal. Globalization is part of our kingdom destiny. We see it in the growing ethnic, cultural, and international diversity of our campus. We also hope to see it in growing partnerships with Christians in other places: leaders in ministry and education who can benefit from our history, while at the same time offering us the vitality of their faith, the strength of their suffering, and the courage of their theological convictions.

We can also expect this: opposition to our kingdom work will grow. Any wise consideration of our culture will confirm that biblical principles of thought and Christian standards of behavior are under duress. In a post-Christian society, tolerance toward people who follow Christ is turning toward antagonism. Nowhere is this more apparent than in higher

education, where Christianity is often viewed as the historic enemy of intellectual progress.

But even if this were not true—even if the Christian worldview maintained a prevailing influence on academia and American life—we would still expect increasing opposition to everything that Wheaton represents. The kingdom of Jesus Christ is never uncontested; the followers of Christ are always compelled to carry the cross. Just as the world hated our Lord, so it will hate us. It will hate our proclamation of absolute truth, our belief in a Creator God, our commitment to sexual purity, and our faith in Jesus as the only way to salvation.

Because the kingdom of Christ is always in conflict, Wheaton College will always need to be, in some measure, a counter-cultural institution. This does not mean that we should withdraw from our culture, as evangelicals were strongly tempted to do throughout the first century of the College. On the contrary, we will continue to seek

cultural transformation along biblical lines, serving the preservative and illuminative functions of salt and light.

Yet for the foreseeable future, the stronger temptation our community faces is to become less and less distinguishable from the world, to serve "the kingdom of self" or "the kingdom of stuff" rather than the kingdom of Christ. This temptation comes from inside the evangelical church as well as outside, from the surrounding culture. Will we have the biblical knowledge and theological discernment to know where to connect with our culture and where to counter it?

It will be hard for Wheaton to stay on its kingdom course. Our Statement of Faith can help us—not as a sterile set of doctrines, but as a living affirmation of our faith in God, in the truth of His Word and the gospel of His Son. Our Community Covenant can help us, too—not as a list of rules, but as an alternative way of life that is shaped by the Cross and empowered by the empty tomb.

"Let us go forward, therefore, with maximum optimism, trusting God, committed to Jesus Christ as Lord, in no way deterred by problems that plague such schools as ours, or paralyzed by fearful events that loom large on the horizon of our lives. Rather, let the historians write of us that our singular praise was to have done the best things in the worst times."

—Dr. Gerald F. Hawthorne '51, M.A. '54, *Professor of New Testament Greek and Exegesis, 1982*

Our ultimate confidence is not in the strength of our own promises and convictions, however, but only in the saving and sanctifying grace of the Father, the Son, and the Holy Spirit. The Triune God is at work in a rising generation of women and men who have extraordinary opportunities to show the world what a difference it makes to live for Christ.

We also know this about the future: everything that is truly done for Christ and His kingdom will endure. This is true for every academic discipline. It is true for the discoveries of science, the melodies of music, and the images of literature. It is true for the social and political sciences, for medicine and mathematics, for theology and archeology, for philosophy and the arts. It is also true for what happens outside the classroom—in the dorm room, on the practice field, at the Stupe, and also in Edman Chapel.

Whatever we do for Jesus is part of His kingdom work. It is all part of what President Blanchard described as "preparing the way for His coming." Indeed, it is part of Christ's kingdom itself, for wherever Christ is honored, His rule is established.

At 150 years, and counting, the College is well known for its commitment to Christian liberal arts education. One of the best descriptions of our primary task comes from an essay ("Of Education") by the epic poet and Christian visionary John Milton, in which he defined a liberal education as one that "fits a man to perform justly, skillfully, and magnanimously all the offices, both private and public, of peace and war." This is the genius of an education in the liberal arts: rather than enabling its students to do nothing in particular, it prepares them for anything and everything. Wheaton students, faculty, staff, and alumni prove this every day in the thousands of kingdom places where they serve.

A properly Christian education does something more: it helps to prepare us for the end of the world. As Arthur Holmes '50, M.A. '52 has written,

"Christian liberal arts education has an eternity in view." It readies us for the day when "the kingdom of this world" will become "the kingdom of our Lord and of his Christ" (Rev. 11:15, NIV).

We are looking forward to that great day. It is part of our eschatology, our hopeful expectation for the future. John Milton had the same hope, and at the end of his *Animadversions*, he took our longing for the Christ of the kingdom and turned it into musical prose:

> Thy kingdom is now at hand, and thou standing at the door. Come forth out of thy royal chambers, O Prince of all the kings of the earth! Put on the visible robes of thy imperial majesty, take up that unlimited scepter which thy Almighty Father hath bequeathed thee; for now the voice of thy bride calls thee, and all creatures sigh to be renewed.

Come, Lord Christ, and with your kingdom, come!

A President's Prayer
Dr. Hudson T. Armerding

Lord, we thank you again that we can call upon you.

And so I ask for my dear friends who work, study, and serve at Wheaton College—who are very close to you, O Lord—that during the Sesquicentennial celebration, they would look at the unique truths, history, and principles that make up Wheaton College.

Grant that those who have loved and served at Wheaton for many decades will be given a sense of ministry to be useful for growing in grace. Help them be part of that which you yourself, O Lord, have established for us.

And, dear Lord, I pray for Wheaton's faculty and students, that as they come to Wheaton they will be strengthened in their faith because of the prayer and work of those who have gone before.

And so, Lord, I thank you for the blessings of the past to Wheaton. You are so gracious. You helped me, Lord, through some very difficult times when I served as Wheaton's president, and I pray that this would be true of those who follow, until Christ returns.

And Lord, until that time comes, your power and your direction will enable us to bring glory to your name, and blessing to those whom we would bring before you for help and strength. I pray for all those who are part of the Wheaton College community, present and future. Please give them strength and encouragement and a sense of realizing that what matters ultimately and eternally, is not so much their views but yours as made known in your Holy Scriptures.

I pray your special grace and protection on all these dear ones who study and work at Wheaton, praying with thanksgiving through Jesus Christ our Lord.

Amen.

His prayer, July 22, 2008. Dr. Armerding '41 entered the presence of the Lord he served so faithfully and for so long on December 1, 2009, at 91 years of age.

A President's Prayer
Dr. J. Richard Chase

Father God, you have given a high calling to the people of Wheaton College, a college whose soul breathes "For Christ and His Kingdom." Such a soul demands excellence in the design of our offerings, so cleanse our hearts and create in us obedience to your Spirit of truth. It demands the best craftsmen, scholars, and leaders, so we look to you to provide these individuals now and as Wheaton's future unfolds.

Aspiring to be and do all things "For Christ and His Kingdom" demands reverence for you. We do reverence you for endowing your creation with mystery, and humankind with the capability for responsible thought and enriching commitments.

We thank you for sending students to Wheaton, men and women from all over the world, who share a love for your Son and want to help build His kingdom. We pray that Wheaton's scholars and teachers will remain rooted and grounded in you; and that their students not only may acquire the knowledge to be found in scholarship and learning, but also be prepared for life on a foundation of lasting values that you have revealed through your Word.

We give thanks for faculty and administrators who, for 150 years, have been committed to Christ-centered higher education. They have been instrumental in helping to form the mind of Christ in these students. May this marvelous work continue until Christ returns.

You have greatly blessed this College, Father. We ask for your hand of blessing on it for all the years to come, and that we will be faithful in giving you the glory.

In the precious name of your Son, Jesus Christ, we pray.

Amen.

WHEATON COLLEGE SESQUICENTENNIAL ANNIVERSARY

The years Ruth and I spent at Wheaton College were among the most important of our lives, and I will always be grateful for the way God used my time there to expand my knowledge and give me a greater understanding of what it means to live "For Christ and His Kingdom."

Our world has changed since Ruth and I graduated and were married 65 years ago—and has changed even more since Wheaton's founding 150 years ago. Nor will the world 65 or 150 years from now be the same as it is today. Only God knows what new challenges and opportunities future generations of Wheaton students may face.

But no matter how much our world changes, I pray that every student who comes to Wheaton will seek to build his or her life on those things that do not change. God does not change, and neither do the truth and authority of His Word. Neither has the gospel changed—the good news that God has come down to us in the person of His only Son, Jesus Christ, who by His death and resurrection has conquered sin and death and hell. Nor does Christ's call change—the call to commit our lives to Him in repentance and faith, and to become His followers in the power of the Holy Spirit. Nor do the spiritual needs of our world change—a world that has lost its way, and is in desperate need of discovering the hope and new life God offers us in Christ.

One hundred fifty years ago Wheaton's founders had one goal: To be faithful to Jesus Christ. My prayer is that this will be the goal of every student and every faculty member who becomes part of this unique community in the future. May God continue to bless Wheaton College, and use it in even greater ways to reach our world for Christ.

Warmly,

Billy Graham

Acknowledgments

PROJECT TEAM Myrna Grant M.A. '71, Associate Professor Emerita, Editor; Georgia Irwin Douglass '70, M.A. '94, Director of Marketing Communications; Marcy Hintz M.A. '08, Sesquicentennial Coordinator, Writer; Alanna Foxwell-Barajas '06, Writer, Assistant Editor

ESSAYISTS "Prologue," Myrna Grant M.A. '71; "Our Purpose," Duane Litfin; "Our Story," Mark A. Noll '68; "Our Faculty," Jill Peláez Baumgaertner; "Our Campus," Samuel A. Shellhamer; "Our Alumni," Marilee A. Melvin '72; "Our Future," Philip G. Ryken '88

BOOK DESIGNER Ellen Rising Morris, Eighth Day Creations

PHOTOS AND ART Michael Hudson '89, William Koechling '72, Carlos Vergara '82, Jim Whitmer '69, Walter Danylak, Ellen Rising Morris, Les Barker, Craig Taylor, Rich Nickel, Greg Thompson, Kristen Gillette '10, Robert Walsh, Lynette Holm Hoppe M.A. '89, Ari Hyde '10, Michael Johnson, Elisa Leberis, Laurie Eve Loftin

HISTORICAL CONSULTANTS Wheaton College Archives and Special Collections: David Malone M.A. '92, Keith Call, David Osielski. Billy Graham Center Archives: Wayne Weber, Noel Collins Pfeifer '04

EDITORIAL ADVISORS R. Mark Dillon, Marilee A. Melvin '72

RESEARCH ASSISTANCE Brett Marhanka, Katherine Halberstadt Anderson '90, Michaelangelo Campos '12, Nancy Frey, Linda MacKillop, Cindy Hoidas, Sarah Jane Holsteen '05, Steve Ivester,

Gary LaVanchy '98, Maggie Laya, Elisa Leberis, Mary Haddock, H. Wilbert Norton, Sr. '36, Ray Smith '54, Barbara Watson

REVIEW AND DESIGN SUPPORT Lori Hart, Donna Antoniuk, Melissa Coleman, Laurie Eve Loftin, Nancy Nehmer, Kimberly Post, Mary Leiser, LaTonya Taylor, Ruby Thomas

THE SESQUICENTENNIAL EXECUTIVE COMMITTEE Duane Litfin, Mark Dillon, Georgia I. Douglass '70, M.A. '94, Marcy Hintz M.A. '08, David Maas '62, David Malone M.A. '92, Stephen Mead, Marilee A. Melvin '72, Rodney Sisco '84, Cindra Stackhouse Taetzsch '82

COMMUNITY RESOURCES Center for History: Alberta Adamson, Sally Garrison, Jane Rio; DuPage County Historical Museum: Sara Arnas, Sara Buttita

SPECIAL THANKS Tyndale House Publishers: Mark Taylor, C. J. Van Wagner, Linda Walz '86, Dean Renninger, Bonne Steffen '74

Printed References

Paul Bechtel, *Wheaton College: A Heritage Remembered* (Shaw, 1984); Charles Blanchard 1870, *The Autobiography of Charles A. Blanchard* (1915); Keith Call, *Images of America: Wheaton* (Arcadia, 2006); Edward Coray '23, *The Wheaton I Remember* (Books for Living, 1974); David Howard '49, M.A. '52, *From Wheaton to the Nations* (Wheaton, 2001); David Maas, *Marching to the Drumbeat of Abolitionism: Wheaton College in the Civil War* (Wheaton, 2010); Jean Moore, *Wheaton: A Pictorial History* (Bradley, 1994) and *DuPage at 150 and Those Who Shaped Our World* (1989); W. W. Willard, *Fire on the Prairie* (Van Kampen, 1950)

Chapter Art

Our Purpose

Blanchard Tower. Digital drawing, 2007

MARTY VOELKER, intrigued by the iconic quality of architectural landmarks, intends to capture the long history of these structures in a single, timeless moment with his art. A long-time resident of Wheaton and married to a Wheaton alumna (Natalie Schmidt '88), he passes Blanchard Hall on a daily basis, and his children play on the front lawn and ride bikes down the sidewalk in front of the College. For his family, this image represents community—past, present, and future.

Our Story

Wheaton College. Watercolor, circa 1861
(10 x 14 inches)

What can be read of the artist's name is simply "APGAR." The two structures depicted in the painting stood on the campus of Wheaton College's forerunner, the Illinois Institute. The Main Building (right) now comprises the central portion of Blanchard Hall. The other building (left) was the Ruth Nutting House, possibly the boardinghouse built in 1865 by Rev. Lucius

Matlack, president of the Illinois Institute from 1855-59. This treasured watercolor is displayed in the Blanchard Hall of today, in the President's Office.

Our Faculty

Dr. Clyde S. Kilby. Oil on canvas, 1987
(35 x 32 inches)

DEBORAH MELVIN BEISNER was commissioned by Leanne Payne '71, M.A. '75 to paint this portrait of Dr. Clyde S. Kilby, a Wheaton professor from 1935-1977, and founder and curator of the Marion E. Wade Center from 1965-1981. Dr. Kilby was chair of the English department for 16 years and a prolific author, as well as a leading authority on C. S. Lewis and J. R. R. Tolkien. Out of his personal letters from Lewis and unflagging efforts to preserve the legacy of seven British authors, the Wade Center was established. Dr. Kilby's giftedness shone in the classroom where his twinkling humor and scholarly rigor endeared him to generations of students.

Our Campus

Wheaton Athletics. Acrylics, 2000
(30 x 40 inches)

The artist, RON MAZELLAN '82, played varsity football at Wheaton and is now a professor at Indiana Wesleyan University and a freelance illustrator. His painting was commissioned by the athletics department in 2000 to help commemorate a century of athletics at the College. The work is on display in Eckert Hall of the Sports and Recreation Complex, one of the campus' centers for student life and activity.

Our Alumni

Alumni Mural. Oil on Canvas, 2005
(38 x 8 feet)

HAROLD SUDMAN, of Chicago, completed this mural in 2005, now displayed on a wall in the Todd M. Beamer Memorial Student Center. It was a gift to Wheaton students from alumni, particularly the classes of 1949, 1950, 1959, and 1979. The complete mural includes pictures of Blanchard Hall, two iconic Wheaton presidents, notable alumni and professors, campus landmarks, the College seal, and artifacts from the Wade Center and the Special Collections.

Our Future

Blanchard Hall. Acrylics, 1987
(15 x 20 inches)

MICHAEL ANDERSON '91 painted this impressionistic version of Blanchard Hall when he was a Wheaton student. This piece appeared on the cover of the 1988 *Tower* yearbook. Blanchard Hall was constructed in five sections between 1852 and 1927; the wings, tower, and basement are all additions to the original structure. The constant additions resulted in a labyrinth of twelve different floor levels, many stairwells, dead end corridors, hidden windows, and sagging ceilings. Finally in 1989 Blanchard Hall was gutted and completely renovated. More than 264 tons of stone were removed from inner walls, 65 tons of steel added for reinforcement, and all 317 windows (each a different size) were removed and re-fitted with custom thermal frames.

PRESIDENTIAL PORTRAITS (pages 16-23) Jonathan Blanchard: painted by J. Phillips of the Hudson River School, dated December 27, 1872. Charles Blanchard: painted by DeWitt Whistler Jayne '36. J. Oliver Buswell, Jr.: painted by DeWitt Whistler Jane '36. V. Raymond Edman: photographic portrait by Orlin Kohli, who also taught chemistry at Wheaton in 1920. Hudson T. Armerding: photographic portrait by Orlin Kohli. J. Richard Chase: painted by Joseph Francis Flynn. Duane Litfin: painted by William Chambers, 2008

Given the task of surveying 150 years of Wheaton's history for a commemorative book, the editors knew that much more would have to be left out than put in. We have aimed to give a representation of the sweep of the College's history. For all the beloved people, places, and events that do not appear in this book, we apologize, believing readers will continue to hold their memories dear.